A Rainbow Book

WILLS —
The Big Myth

What You Don't Know Can Hurt Your Family

ROBERT M. DUNN
and
JOAN F. DORFMAN

Rainbow Books, Inc.
FLORIDA

Library of Congress Cataloging-In-Publication Data

Dunn, Robert M., 1949-
  Wills—the big myth : what you don't know can hurt your family / Robert M. Dunn and Joan F. Dorfman.
    p. cm.
  Includes bibliographical references and index.
    ISBN 1-56825-091-6 (trade softcover : alk. paper)
  1. Wills—United States—Popular works. 2. Estate planning—United States—Popular works. I. Dorfman, Joan F., 1949- II. Title.
    KF755.Z9 D86 2002
      346.7305'4—dc21
                                                              2002013805

Published by
Rainbow Books, Inc.
P. O. Box 430,
Highland City, FL 33846-0430

Editorial Offices and Wholesale/Distributor Orders
Telephone: (863) 648-4420
Email: RBIbooks@aol.com

Individuals' Orders
Toll-free Telephone (800) 431-1579
http://www.AllBookStores.com

∞The paper used in this publication meets the minimum requirements of the American National Standard for Information Sciences—Permanence of Paper for Printed Library Materials, ANSI Z39.48-1984.

First edition 2004
10 09 08 07 06 05 04   5 4 3 2 1
Printed in the United States of America

In memory of our
fathers, Louis Dorfman
and David Dunn.

Contents

Notes About Style

If you're like us, you don't like flipping to the back of the book every time you encounter an unfamiliar term. That's why wherever possible, we tried to define estate planning terms in the main body of our book. For ease of reference, they also appear in the glossary.

Our choice of male or female gender for the pronouns referring to spouses, children, attorneys, financial advisors, and the like, is solely for the purpose of making the book easier to read.

Throughout this book we use the words property and assets interchangeably. Your property is not just land, but all the things you own.

Acknowledgments

Many thanks to attorneys Robert Esperti, Reno Peterson, Cliff Rice, and Rob Goldman. Their estate planning ideas have been helpful to us.

We are grateful to Chuck KinCannon, Esq., David Pollan, Esq., Alan Dinerman, CLU, and Greg Long CLU, who read portions of the book and provided thoughtful comments. We express our sincere appreciation to our friend Mary Weidemeyer for her many suggestions in making the difficult concepts expressed in this book more readable.

We also want to acknowledge our editor, Betsy Lampe, and our publisher, Betty Wright. Without their professional expertise and advice this project would not have been possible.

Introduction

You've heard it so often and with such authority that you assume it must be true: If you want to protect your family, then you need a *Will* and life insurance. This time honored advice is the Big Myth. You have peace of mind only because you never considered what can go wrong. Long after you're gone, your family will have to bear the consequences of the *estate planning* decisions (good and bad) that you make today.

In the following pages, you will be learning about Wills — their function and their limitations. We will describe common problems that many families have faced. In each of these circumstances, a Will wasn't sufficient to protect family members, even with the addition of life insurance.

After exposing the big myth (i.e., that Wills and life insurance protect your family), we will focus on other common myths that are associated with the field of estate planning. Our intent is to dispel common misconceptions that impede effective planning.

If you already have a Will, you may remember the feeling of

relief you experienced when you signed it. But do you recall why you had a Will prepared in the first place, and what it was that you hoped to accomplish? If you are like most people, the only discussion was about the people you want to leave your property to and the name of your children's guardian. It was as if those were the only two possible goals available for consideration. The unspoken assumption was that a Will would provide whatever you expected.

If you've met with an attorney to have a Will prepared, did the attorney ask, "What are your estate planning goals?" Did he explain the broad range of goals from which you could choose? Probably not. And that explains why most people end up with what their attorney or financial advisor prescribes. It's a hit or miss proposition as to whether your Will meets your expectations. This is the major problem with estate planning today. It doesn't have to be that way. You can have an estate plan that will do what you want it to do.

There is an old *Saturday Night Live* skit about a short-order restaurant. Everyone who sits down at the counter looks at a menu. No matter what the customers try to order, the cooks tell them that they are out of it. Instead they steer them into ordering a cheeseburger. Everyone gets a cheeseburger at that restaurant, whether they want one or not.

It isn't that much different in estate planning today, with one big exception: you aren't even given a menu. Your advisors (e.g., attorney, CPA, insurance agent, and stockbroker) assume that you want and need a Will. They think they're helping you by telling you to go get a Will or have your existing one updated. Your advisors don't even know that your family can be harmed by their advice!

The question isn't whether a Will, in and of itself, is a good or bad thing. The real question is this: Given what you want to do for yourself and your family, is a Will the right choice for you? We're going to help you answer this question.

Law students graduate with only a basic knowledge of Wills. Twenty years later they may not know much more about Wills than you do. They perpetuate their traditional approach to estate planning which ignores what can go wrong. The solutions presented in this book are legal, but not well known even among lawyers. Many lawyers hate what we have to say because it isn't what they were taught, and they are unwilling to change.

Armed with the concepts presented here, you will have the basic knowledge you need to begin estate planning for your family. You will be able to communicate to your attorney, in very specific terms, what it is that you hope to accomplish. Your attorney can then choose the appropriate tools that are likely to make your hopes a reality, rather than wishful thinking. You will no longer be limited to blind faith in the power of Wills.

R.M.D.
J.F.D.

ONE

Wills: Who's In Control?

What is the purpose of a Will?

A Will is a legal document to dispose of the property *you own* at your death. Your property can include your:

- Personal residence, vacation home
- Rental property
- Cars and boats
- Checking, savings, and money market accounts
- Stocks and bonds
- Furniture
- Jewelry
- Collections such as art, stamp, and coin

Your Will probably controls a whole lot less of your property than you think.

You may be surprised to find out that on your death, your Will doesn't determine who will receive your major assets including your:

- Life insurance
- *IRA, 401(k) account*, or other retirement plans
- Brokerage accounts
- Bank accounts
- Home

There are two major reasons why this occurs. First, your beneficiary designations determine who gets your life insurance proceeds and the remaining balance in your IRA or other retirement plans; and second, you may have property that is owned jointly with another person (usually your spouse).

Beneficiary designations usually cause your property to pass outside your Will.

When you designate a *person*, other than your *estate*, as beneficiary of your life insurance, IRA, or 401(k) account, your Will is not going to control that property. Instead, upon your death, these assets pass outside your Will directly to your beneficiary, under contract law.

If your estate were the beneficiary of your life insurance, IRA or 401(k) account, after your death these assets would be paid into your *probate estate*, where your creditors would feast on them. Life insurance, 401(k) accounts and, in many states, IRAs are free from the claims of creditors unless you make the mistake of naming your estate as beneficiary. This is a common mistake made with life insurance, but made less frequently with 401(k) accounts and IRAs.

Property you own jointly with another person (as joint tenants with right of survivorship) is not controlled by your Will.

You probably weren't even involved in the decision about how to own your property. Your banker, real estate agent, and stockbroker, usually without asking you, simply decided that you and your spouse should own property as *joint tenants with right of survivorship*. On a stock brokerage account statement this is often indicated as *JTWROS*. Wills don't control this property because on the death of the first spouse, the property automatically passes to the surviving spouse, under state law.

Peace of mind is only an illusion.

Wills that do not control your major assets are, for all practical purposes, useless pieces of paper. The peace of mind you get from such a document is merely an illusion, because these Wills do little to accomplish your goals.

If your goal is to leave all your assets to your spouse and children, your Will and life insurance offer no guarantees. As you will see in the following chapter, the problem with leaving property directly to your spouse — and ultimately to your children — is that the assets may never get to your children or be used for the purposes you intended. The outcome depends on chance. Under the best of circumstances you will achieve your desired result. But real life seldom follows a well-crafted script.

In the chapters that follow you will see what can go wrong with Will/life insurance planning, and how you can guarantee that your assets reach your loved ones and are protected for them.

TWO

What Can Go Wrong?

Nobody wakes up in the morning and decides, today I'm going to be hit by a DUI driver, have a fatal heart attack, or be diagnosed with a terminal illness. That's why we do not feel any urgency to plan for the eventuality that someday we will no longer be here. That's why we do not spend sufficient time developing a well-crafted plan. That's why we end up with a Will that plans for the best, rather than the worst.

What follows are examples of some of the problems families can face. They are drawn from real-life stories. The circumstances may seem familiar to you. These stories are not intended to illustrate every problem you can possibly encounter; rather, they will give you an indication of what often goes wrong. The stories show that Wills may not be the all-purpose solutions they're cracked up to be.

PART 1
Mary & John's Story

Just the facts.

Mary and John are both 35 years old, and they have two young sons. John has a *401(k) plan* at work that is currently worth $25,000, and they own their $150,000 home in joint tenancy with right of survivorship. Their home mortgage is $120,000. John recently purchased a $250,000 *term life insurance* policy naming Mary as the primary beneficiary and his children as the contingent beneficiaries. John's 401(k) plan has the same beneficiary designations.

Mary and John recently signed their Wills, leaving their assets to the surviving spouse, and if neither spouse is living, in trust for their children. A copy of John's Will is in Appendix A. It is a typical Will for a young, married father.

What is disturbing about Mary and John's story? There doesn't seem to be anything wrong with what they did.

**Their Wills and life insurance don't guarantee that
any of their assets will ever get to their children.**

Mary and John intended to have their assets get to their children, but their assets just as easily might not. The lawyer who wrote their Wills didn't tell them it was a *maybe*. He didn't say, "John if you die first, your Will is a worthless piece of paper. It doesn't control the disposition of any property. All of your property is going to pass outside your Will: Your house passes to Mary because it is titled in *joint tenancy with right of survivorship* (i.e., the share of the first spouse to die automatically passes, by law, to the surviving spouse). And your 401(k) plan and life insurance pass to Mary because she is the designated beneficiary."

The lawyer didn't tell John that, by having the life insurance proceeds and other assets go directly to Mary at his death, the stage was set for Mary to inadvertently lose the assets and disinherit their children. The following describes a variety of ways that can occur.

What can go wrong.

Scenario 1: After John's death, Mary remarries and places her assets in a stock brokerage account titled jointly with right of survivorship.

John died in a car accident; Mary remarried and put the life insurance proceeds into a stock brokerage account. Mary always held everything jointly with John, and she automatically did the same with her new husband, Matt. Their brokerage account was titled, "Mary Martin & Matt Martin, JTWROS." Mary never paid attention to the name on the account, and she could not have told you that *JTWROS* means joint tenancy with right of survivorship. When Mary died of cancer 10 years later, all of the brokerage account went to Matt. None of the stock ever got to her children.

Scenario 2: The new husband has a cash flow problem in his business.

After John's death Mary conscientiously put all of the life insurance proceeds into her own account. A number of years later, her new husband, Matt, said, "Mary I'm having a temporary cash flow problem in our construction business. Can I borrow fifty thousand dollars until the next project is completed?" As a loving wife, Mary made the loan. Unfortunately, Matt's business continued to have cash flow problems, and he was never able to repay what he borrowed.

Scenario 3: Mary has an unexpected creditor.

The corporation minutes of Matt's construction company named Mary as Secretary/Treasurer. A downturn in the economy caused the business to have a serious cash flow problem. Matt failed to pay $50,000 of employee withholding tax. According to Internal Revenue Code Sections 6671(b) and 6672, officers and employees in a position of financial responsibility are personally liable for the payment of employee withholding tax. Mary was forced to use over $50,000 of John's life insurance money to pay the tax and penalties for Matt's business.

Scenario 4: The children receive their inheritance, but
lose it to a failed marriage or an unexpected creditor.

Mary lived to age 75 and left $400,000 worth of cash and securities to her two sons, in equal shares as stated in her Will. What could not be foreseen, were the unexpected circumstances in which Mary's two sons would lose their inheritance.

Mary's eldest son invested his inheritance in his stock brokerage account that he jointly owned with his wife. Unfortunately, his marriage later ended in divorce. Half of his assets, including his inheritance that he put into the joint account, went to his wife under the terms of the divorce settlement.

Mary's second son owned a metals salvage yard. He paid $2,500 to have some bus batteries removed from the yard. Without his knowledge, the batteries were dumped in a Florida lake that later became an EPA Superfund Site. The EPA obtained a $1 million judgment against him and his corporation for Superfund cleanup.

Mary and John's children are left
unprotected in other ways.

Mary and John's Wills contain no
instructions for the care of their two sons.

Let's change the facts and assume that Mary and John died in a fire at a Las Vegas hotel, while their sons were still in pre-school. With them died all their hopes, dreams and aspirations for their children, because their appointed guardian had no knowledge of their wishes.

John had played baseball at Georgia Tech, where Mary's father is a professor. John wanted his sons to play as much baseball as possible while growing up. Mary wanted her sons to have a private school education like she had. There were many instructions on the raising of their sons that they would have wanted to tell their children's guardian. But the reality was that their instructions were never expressed in writing.

Mary's sister (the guardian named in John and Mary's Wills) lives in a small house and has two children of her own. Mary would have liked her sons to have their own separate rooms and make education a top priority in their lives. John would have wanted his sons to spend some time each summer with his parents on their farm, outside of Louisville, Kentucky. Mary would have also wanted her sons to be encouraged to play a musical instrument and to be given lessons if they showed an interest. She would have liked to tell her sister, "I don't want my sons to go to just *any* college, but rather to one that is tops in the country. And if my children want to obtain advanced degrees, encourage them to obtain that, too, from a school that is premier in that particular field of study." Mary wanted her sons to be supervised each day after school, either studying or playing sports. While in high school she would have liked them to work during the summers and Christmas vacations. Mary also would have wanted to give her sons money for a modest wedding, to start a business, and for a down payment on a home.

Mary and John wrote their Wills so that, in case of their untimely deaths, their children would be taken care of. Nobody pointed out to them that they didn't give any instructions to the guardian for the care of their children. Nobody knew any of Mary and John's wishes because they were never put in writing.

Mary and John's insurance was insufficient
to accomplish their goals.

If Mary and John's insurance agent or attorney had encouraged them to write down instructions for their children's care, Mary and John would have seen for themselves that their $250,000 term policy was completely inadequate to provide for private school, baseball teams, trips to visit the grandparents, music lessons, top colleges and graduate schools, weddings, starting a business, down payments on homes, etc. The $250,000 life insurance policy would have been used up before the children finished the 10th grade.

Mary and John give the local probate court judge (i.e., a total stranger) control of their children's well being and finances.

As is common practice, John named Mary primary beneficiary and his minor children as alternate beneficiaries of his $250,000 life insurance policy. He also did the same thing with his 401(k) plan.

Since Mary died in the Las Vegas hotel fire along with John, their two sons became the beneficiaries of the insurance policy. Insurance companies will not pay life insurance proceeds directly to a minor but instead require a "guardian of the property" (in some states this person is called a "conservator") to be appointed by the local probate court.

The legal process required Mary's sister to petition the probate court to be appointed guardian. On the petition, Mary's sister correctly stated that she will have $275,000 of cash assets under her care — the life insurance plus the 401(k) plan. After Mary's sister spent several thousand dollars to purchase a $275,000 insurance bond, the court appointed her "guardian of the person and property."

Whatever Mary and John had in mind for the $250,000 of insurance proceeds, it will not be up to them or to Mary's sister. The probate court judge will decide upon all disbursements until a child is 18. An exception to this is the interest income earned on the guardianship funds. This income in most states can be spent without the judge's approval.

Mary and John wanted Mary's sister to be the guardian of their two sons, but they left her no instructions for the care of their children. Mary and John inadvertently put a stranger (the probate court judge) in control of the disbursement of all funds. The reality of the probate court guardianship system is that principal is preserved as much as possible. At age 18 each child will receive his share of the funds. Mary and John would not have wanted their sons to be given a large sum of money at age 18 because those funds needed to be protected for college. Mary and John would never have trusted their sons to be mature enough to responsibly manage a large sum of money, without supervision, at age 18.

PART 2
Mrs. Smith's Story

Just The Facts.

Mrs. Smith is 85 years old. She has two children who are married and have families of their own. Her husband, Sam, died 10 years ago. She owns a $150,000 house, with no mortgage, and has $150,000 worth of stocks.

She goes to see a lawyer and says, "I want to put my house and stocks jointly in my name and my children's names. I want it set up so that if I become disabled they can use my assets to take care of me. And when I die, I want my assets to go to my children without going through probate."

Her attorney replies, "That sounds like a pretty good idea. I can prepare a deed putting your house in joint tenancy with right of survivorship. I can also write a letter for you to send to your stockbroker telling him to do the same with your stocks."

What is disturbing about Mrs. Smith's story? There doesn't *seem* to be anything wrong with what she did.

What can go wrong.

Scenario 1: One of Mrs. Smith's children becomes divorced.

After Mrs. Smith titled her house and stocks so that she and her children owned them as "joint tenants with right of survivorship," they each owned all the property with each other. With this type of ownership a creditor of any of them can file a lawsuit and take the entire property to satisfy the debt. One of Mrs. Smith's children becomes divorced, and Mrs. Smith's home and stocks become part of the divorce settlement.

Scenario 2: Mrs. Smith's son falls behind in paying his bills and gets sued for $7500.

Mrs. Smith's son is a joint owner of her house. Her home becomes subject to a creditor's lien after a $7,500 judgment is obtained against her son. She can't sell her home and move to Arizona, to live with her sister, without first satisfying the lien.

Scenario 3: Mrs. Smith has an unexpected creditor.

Mrs. Smith's son accidentally breaks a pedestrian's hip in an auto accident which he caused. When the hip heals 10 months later, the pedestrian has a permanent limp. The son has $50,000 of auto insurance but gets sued by the pedestrian for $300,000. The son then files for bankruptcy. Mrs. Smith's home becomes one of the assets her son must declare in his bankruptcy proceedings.

Scenario 4: Mrs. Smith wants to sell her home and move away, but her children don't want her to.

Mrs. Smith breaks her leg after slipping on her stairs. No longer able to live on her own, Mrs. Smith wants to sell her house and move to Phoenix to share a home with her sister. Her daughter doesn't want her to move, because it will be too difficult to take care of her mother in Phoenix. Mrs. Smith can't sell her home without getting each child to sign the deed.

PART 3

Rose's Story

Just the facts.

George, age 60, has been married for 25 years to Rose, age 50. Like his father before him, George controlled all the family finances. The house, bank accounts, investments, etc., were all titled in his name. George paid all of the bills out of his own money-market checking account. He would transfer, monthly, a small sum of money to Rose's regular checking account, so that she would have funds for groceries and incidental expenses. George had a Will leaving all his property to Rose.

What can go wrong.

Scenario 1: A sudden disability causes George to relinquish all financial control to a total stranger, the probate court judge.

Shortly after New Year's, George had a severe stroke that left him unable to speak and a quadriplegic. He needed constant, full time medical attention. The outlook for his recovery was poor.

Rose had no way to access her husband's accounts to pay the mortgage, grocery bills and medical expenses. She had to hire an attorney to petition the probate court for her to become her husband's guardian of the property (conservator). Only after being appointed guardian of the property did Rose have the legal authority to obtain access to George's accounts in order to pay the mortgage and household expenses.

Rose was stunned when the judge told her that George's assets belonged to George, and that she could not spend any of the guardianship assets on herself, even to buy clothes and make-up, without the judge's permission. Rose had always thought that all the assets acquired during their marriage, belonged to her and George. She couldn't believe that a total stranger, the probate court judge, now controlled all their wealth.

Scenario 2: George's bank and stock brokerage company refuse to honor his durable power of attorney.

Before his disability, George prepared a *durable power of attorney* naming Rose as his agent. George intended for Rose, as his agent, to be able to access to his bank and investment accounts without having to get involved with the probate court.

George's durable power of attorney, however, did not guarantee Rose access to George's assets. Quite often, as in this case, banks and brokerage companies refuse to honor durable powers of attorney. Banks and brokerage companies don't like dealing with agents. There is too much potential liability for them, because an agent is not the legal owner of the account.

PART 4

Linda's Story

Just the facts.

Linda is 50 years old and divorced. Her daughter is a college junior. Linda has a terminal illness and is comforted only by the thought that her $25,000 life insurance policy will be just enough for her daughter to complete college. Linda owns no other assets.

Linda is appreciative when a family friend, who is a well-known estate planning attorney, offers to prepare her Will for free. She explains to him that the insurance proceeds are to be left in a trust for her daughter's college education. Linda believes that her daughter would not use the $25,000 to finish college if she received the $25,000 directly.

What can go wrong.

The attorney arranges for Linda to name
her estate as beneficiary of the $25,000 insurance policy.

The attorney included in Linda's Will an education trust for Linda's daughter. The attorney arranged for Linda to change the beneficiary of the insurance policy from her daughter's name to "the estate of the insured." The idea was for the insurance proceeds to be paid to Linda's *executor* who would then put the money into the education trust that is included in her Will.

Soon after Linda's death, the executor received the $25,000 insurance check. However, after paying Linda's debts, which consisted mostly of unpaid medical bills, only $2,500 was left for the education trust.

This is a classic mistake that is often made. Insurance proceeds are free from claims of creditors unless "the executor" or "the estate of the insured" is foolishly named as beneficiary.

PART 5
Elaine's Story

Just the facts.

Elaine, an 82-year-old widow, recently moved into an assisted living home. Her only asset is a $300,000 money market account that she inherited from her husband. Elaine's Will leaves her assets equally to her two children, Sam and Diane, whom she loves very much. Sam, a bartender, has a history of being financially irresponsible. On the other hand, Diane has always been just the opposite and extremely trustworthy. Diane does not like her brother and rarely speaks to him.

What can go wrong.

Elaine unintentionally disinherits her son.

Elaine, due to her failing health, no longer wants the responsibility of paying her monthly bills. She asks Diane to take over this job and adds Diane's name to the money market account and signature card.

Elaine doesn't realize that by creating the joint money market account she set in motion the future disinheritance of her son. Under state law, Diane, as the surviving individual on the joint money market account, will become the sole owner. A Will does not control the disposition of a joint checking or money market account. Even though Elaine's Will leaves her assets equally to her children, it will be up to Diane to decide whether or not to share the $300,000 money market account with her brother.

THREE

Common Myths
About Estate Planning

There are a number of myths about estate planning that lull you into believing that all you need to do to protect your family is get a Will and buy some life insurance. In this chapter we'll examine these myths to dispel some common misconceptions that impede effective planning.

Myth 1 — Your Will protects your family.

As we have seen, your Will doesn't control property that passes to an individual named as beneficiary of your life insurance policy, IRA, or 401(k) account. Similarly, upon your death property you own jointly with right of survivorship passes outside of your Will directly to the surviving owner(s). It would not be unusual if your Will controlled virtually none of your property. A Will that doesn't control your property can't protect your family.

Myth 2 — Naming a guardian is sufficient to take care of your minor children.

Your Will is the document that is required, under state law, to name a guardian for your minor children. However, your Will does not provide that guardian with a blueprint on how you want your children raised. Detailed instructions are needed.

You can leave detailed instructions for the care of your minor children in your estate planning documents. (See Appendix C for sample instructions.) It's sad that the average couple leaves more instructions on the care of their children to their baby sitter, than they give to the guardian of their children.

If you are interested in privacy, you may not want to publicly declare your inner most hopes, desires and dreams for your children in your Will. Upon your death, your Will is filed with the probate court. From then on, it is a public document that anyone can read. On the other hand, a *revocable living trust* (a trust that can be changed at any time by the trust maker up until his death) provides a blanket of privacy, away from the scrutiny of the public eye. When you use a revocable living trust as your main estate planning document, your instructions are visible only to those who have a genuine need to know them.

Myth 3 — Your assets have to be paid outright to your loved ones in either one lump sum or at specified age intervals.

Custom dictates that, in your Will, you leave your assets to your loved ones with no strings attached. A common variation is to distribute your children's inheritance at pre-determined age intervals. For example, you may want your child to receive money at the specified ages of 25, 30 and 35. However, when you leave money outright to your loved ones, you lose an opportunity to influence their behavior and to protect them from losing their inheritance.

Suppose you want to leave one third of your estate to each of your three children. Rather than leave your assets outright, you can create separate trusts that come into existence after your death to hold each child's share, tailored to each child's needs.

For example, after your death you can provide incentives for a drug-addicted son to kick his habit, by placing his inheritance in a trust — for his lifetime. If he successfully completes a substance abuse program and remains drug free for three years, he will be given one fourth of everything in his trust as an incentive. He receives another fourth if he stays clean for another five years. The remainder stays in the trust, just in case. The trustee of the trust can be instructed to pay the principal and income out if your son needs it, but directly to the person providing the service or product rather than to your son.

A second trust can protect your youngest daughter, the one who always falls for the wrong guy, from losing her inheritance to a failed marriage. Even your older daughter, the perfect child whom all parents wish they had, can benefit from having her share of your estate placed in a third trust. Although the trust can be written to allow her to get whatever she wants, whenever she wants, the trust will take care of her if she becomes disabled or incapacitated. Her inheritance will also be protected should she ever be sued.

Each child still receives one third of your assets. But you have provided your son with an incentive for adopting a desired lifestyle, and you have created safety nets for all three children.

Although these types of trusts for family members can be part of your Will or revocable living trust, there are good reasons for not making these trusts part of your Will. You may not want to announce to the public, via your Will after probate, the special provisions you have written because your son or daughter has an addiction to drugs, alcohol or gambling, or because your husband is a spendthrift or your wife is addicted to the home shopping network. A revocable living trust keeps these family matters private. Only the trustee of your revocable living trust needs to know the details of your family members' weaknesses, in order to carry out your wishes.

Myth 4 — Probate is no big deal.

Probate is the process of proving the validity of a Will. If you have a Will, state law requires probate of your Will at your death. Probate is needed when a person dies with assets titled in his name.

The deceased is no longer here to sign his name, so that his assets can be legally transferred to his family and other beneficiaries. The probate court judge appoints an executor, who is given the power to transfer the deceased's assets in accordance with the terms of his Will.

Some probate lawyers make their entire livings based on the fees they charge for probating Wills. These attorneys charge a hefty fee to transfer the title of the various assets to the heirs. An additional money maker in their practice is filling out federal *Form 706* (the federal estate tax return) for a taxable estate greater than $1 million (soon to be greater than $3.5 million in 2009, but falling back to $1 million in 2011). If they probate the Will, they will certainly get the Form 706 business.

We sometimes hear attorneys and other professional advisors say that probate is no big deal. However, if a person has numerous assets, probate is a big deal. Probate is an even bigger deal if no one, other than the deceased, knows where all those assets are located.

What might have been easy during the deceased's lifetime becomes a very costly and time-consuming proposition. The probate attorney has to first determine what and where all the assets are. Then he must legally change the title of all those assets to the beneficiaries named in the deceased's Will.

Probate fees could eat up from three percent to nine percent of your *probate estate* (all of a decedent's assets whose disposition is controlled by his Will). It just depends on how much the probate lawyer chooses to charge your family. Probate fees can take a tremendous bite out of your estate — unnecessarily.

Myth 5 — Estate taxes have been repealed.

During the 2000 presidential campaign, President Bush ran on a platform to repeal the estate tax. His proposal received wide-spread support, and Congress, in the *Economic Growth and Tax Relief Act of 2001*, appeared at first glance to go along with the President. The Act significantly reduces estate taxes through 2009, and then repeals the estate tax in 2010. The surprise is that in 2011, the old pre-act law (the law in effect on June 6, 2001) with its higher taxes, is brought back to life. Congress repealed the estate tax for the year 2010 only!

Many members of Congress are continuing their drive to immediately repeal the estate tax, once and for all. So by the time you read this, the estate tax may be a thing of the past.

Even if the estate tax is in effect at the time of your death, with proper planning there are ways to reduce or avoid it. The basics of reducing estate taxes are discussed in Chapter Six, pages 78 through 82. The most common advanced estate savings tools are listed in Chapter Four, page 61.

Myth 6 — There are no consequences for procrastinating in estate planning.

Common wisdom has it that, as long as you are alive and kicking, it's not too late to begin your estate planning, and that your procrastination has little or no effect on the outcome. In actuality, delaying your planning can be a very costly mistake.

Procrastination exacts its toll in three main estate planning areas:

- Purchase of life insurance
- Choice of tools to minimize your estate taxes
- Retirement funds subject to estate and income taxes

In each case, the longer the delay, the greater the cost to your family. For example if your plan requires the use of a *cash value life insurance* policy, the earlier you purchase the life insurance, the lower its annual premium and the lower its total cost. This is because the insurance company will have more time to credit dividends and interest income to your policy and will initially have less risk of you dying. Waiting to purchase life insurance will definitely increase the cost.

The next area where procrastination exacts its toll is the choice of tools available to you to reduce estate taxes. Some tools take effect immediately, and others require time to work. Many of these tools are found in the *Internal Revenue Code* (e.g., the *charitable lead trust*). Other tools, such as the *irrevocable life insurance trust*, have been approved or upheld over the years by the courts. The father who wants to pass his business to his sons without the IRS stealing half the value must start his planning in his forties.

A similar result occurs with retirement plans — IRAs and 401(k) plans — that will one day be subject to estate tax. If this is your situation, you should determine in your forties and fifties whether you are going to spend these assets during your retirement or pass them on to your children at your death (or, if married, at the surviving spouse's death). You'll want to plan early enough to minimize estate taxes imposed on retirement plan assets and to delay income taxes imposed on retirement plan distributions. Purchasing life insurance is a common solution for creating cash to pay future estate taxes, but you don't want to find this out in your later years when the premiums are no longer affordable. The point is to develop a plan for retirement funds early, so that what you want to do can be accomplished without an unexpected tax bite.

Myth 7 — Your life insurance is guaranteed to protect your family.

You're buying life insurance expecting guaranteed premiums (your insurance company can't raise your premiums) and guaranteed death benefits (your insurance company can't lower your death benefits). But many policies don't have these guarantees.

There are two main types of policies – term and those with a cash value. Term insurance protects you for a specific period of time (such as 1, 5, 10, 20 years or until age 65). Term policies guarantee a fixed death benefit for the amount of the policy if you die within the term. The premiums are guaranteed not to change from the amounts stated in the policy. Less than two percent of the people who have ever bought a term policy have actually died during the policy term. This is because term insurance premiums become too expensive at older ages, and people drop their term policies before they die.

Cash value policies are usually sold to provide insurance protection for your lifetime. Most cash value policies are full of surprises, but you won't know about them until years later. The two main generic types of cash value policies are traditional whole life and universal life. Traditional whole life has guaranteed level premiums and a guaranteed death benefit. The insurance company credits dividends (or interest income) to your policy. The amount credited is based on a number of factors, including the company's earnings on investments and payments for death claims and agents' commissions. Your premiums have to be paid every year, but they don't have to be paid in cash. Over the years if the dividends (or interest income) credited to your policy are sufficiently large, you can stop paying cash premiums and the premiums can be taken out of the dividends (or the interest income). Nobody buys whole life expecting to pay every premium in cash. The computerized sales illustration prepared by your agent will show that based on current dividend rates, you will have to pay cash premiums for say only 10 or 12 years, and your premium obligation will "vanish." (This is the vanishing premium sales technique and is used in selling all cash value policies.) The sales illustration will also show that your initial guaranteed death benefit will grow to a much larger amount. However, there is no guarantee that dividends (or interest income) will be credited at the same rate each year or even be paid. So, don't be surprised if you have to keep paying cash premiums much longer than you expected. And don't believe that your death benefit will grow, because an increased death benefit isn't guaranteed either.

With universal life neither the premiums nor the death benefits are guaranteed, making it the riskiest way to provide lifetime insurance coverage. Because there are no guarantees, the premiums are approximately 35% lower than traditional whole life. Universal life policies fall into two categories, regular universal and variable universal. With regular universal life, the insurance company invests your premiums and usually guarantees a 4% return. (The sales illustration that your agent gives you includes an additional column showing a much higher hypothetical return.) Variable universal life differs in that you (rather than the insurance company) direct the investment of your premiums in accounts set up by the insurance company, usually in mutual funds.

Universal life policies pay a death benefit only if your policy has at least one dollar of cash value in it when you die. Cash values increase with premium payments and interest credits, and decrease with charges for company expenses and mortality costs (costs of paying death claims). When buying a universal life policy the following events typically occur: Your insurance agent prepares a sales illustration that calculates the suggested premium for you to pay. The premium will fall within a broad range set by the insurance company (low side) and the Internal Revenue Service (high side). The sales illustration uses the vanishing premium sales technique to show that hypothetically you only have to pay cash premiums for ten or twelve years, or so. If your agent's assumptions in preparing the sales illustration are overly optimistic about interest income, expenses, mortality costs, and how long your policy needs to last, your premiums will be low. If your premiums are too low you will one day receive a letter from the insurance company telling you to pay an unusually large premium or your policy will lapse (go broke). If your policy lapses, your family will not receive any death benefit. A universal life policy shifts the risk of keeping a policy alive from the insurance company to you. It can be a costly gamble that requires a watchful eye.

Universal life's non-guaranteed death benefits are too uncertain for many conservative insurance buyers. Insurance companies are recognizing that there is a market for universal life products that have more guarantees. Some universal life policies currently offer a guaranteed minimum death benefit, when you pay an additional premium. These additional premiums are expensive, and most people probably aren't willing to pay them. In response to consumer demand several companies are introducing universal life products that pay a guaranteed death benefit in exchange for a pre-determined premium.

Myth 8 — In the event of a medical emergency, your hospital will have a copy of your living will and health care power of attorney.

Medical emergencies can occur suddenly at any time of the day or night. You planned for such an event by signing a *living will* and a *health care power of attorney*. (Different states may have different names for these documents.) A living will outlines your wishes regarding the use or non-use of medical treatment to artificially prolong your life. A health care power of attorney designates a person who can make decisions about medical treatment, if you become incapacitated and cannot make your wishes known. (Your state may have standard approved forms for living wills and health care powers of attorney).

A living will and a health care power of attorney are useless to you if they remain tucked away in your home — or worse yet, locked away in your safe deposit box — while you lie in a hospital, unconscious or unable to communicate. In a medical emergency, these documents are only valuable when your hospital has a copy of them.

Ordinarily, people don't carry their living will and health care power of attorney with them. You could pre-arrange with trusted friends or loved ones to safeguard copies of your living will and health care power of attorney. It's not very difficult to carry in your wallet the names and telephone numbers of these people for hospital personnel to call in an emergency situation. Your family members or friends would be responsible for faxing, mailing or hand delivering the documents to your hospital, as needed.

If you want to guarantee that, in an emergency, these documents will be immediately sent to hospital personnel, you could use an electronic health care document storage and retrieval service, such as DocuBank (www.docubank.com). For example, DocuBank stores copies of your living will and health care power of attorney, along with emergency information such as phone numbers of family members and physicians. DocuBank provides an emergency card to carry in your wallet with a toll-free number which a family member or hospital can dial, to have copies of these documents faxed to them, any time of the day or night.

Myth 9 — Your estate is safe in the hands of your family members and attorney.

Some family members and attorneys aren't trustworthy. As executors and trustees they may steal from your estate at your death. Even during your lifetime, the person you appoint as agent of your durable power of attorney can help himself to your money. The elderly are especially at risk for this type of theft. Exercise caution when naming the agent of your durable power of attorney. If you have any doubt about an attorney's or family member's honesty or ability to handle money, don't appoint him your executor, trustee or agent.

If you don't have anyone to fill these roles, what should you do? If you have a large estate, you can name your bank or stock brokerage company to be your executor and/or trustee. A bank or brokerage company may charge high fees, but they won't run off to Las Vegas with your money.

If you have a small estate and you are not sure about the trustworthiness of your possible executors, trustees or agents, then you should actively seek probate or a court appointed guardianship. You can guarantee the probate court's supervision of your estate if you become mentally incapacitated or die, by doing the following:

- Own assets in your own name rather than jointly with someone else

- Refuse to sign a durable power of attorney

- Use a Will rather than a revocable living trust as your main estate planning document

You can give the probate court even more control by stating in your Will that upon your death your executor must purchase an *executor's bond* and file both an *inventory* and an *annual return*. In fact, in many states an executor's bond, an inventory, and an annual return are required to be filed with the probate court, unless the Will says otherwise.

Myth 10 — Family members or friends will take care of your pets if you become incapacitated or die.

For many people, their pets are like members of their family. For still others, their pets are their only family. Many people die believing that their family members or friends will take care of their pets. The reality is that pet caregivers become ill, move or discover that there is a lot more work to caring for pets, than they originally expected. These pets often end up at local animal shelters where they are destroyed. What you can do to protect your pets is discussed in Chapter Ten.

Myth 11 — Medicare and your other insurance will pay for your long-term care.

Long-term care, although it can involve medical care, is mainly *custodial care* that assists a person with the *activities of daily living*: getting out of bed, walking to the bathroom, using the toilet, bathing, eating, and dressing. When you are healthy, you don't think about this kind of assistance. But if you have a stroke or Alzheimer's, you will need full-time assistance in your home, an assisted living center, or a nursing home.

Do you think that Medicare and your other insurance will pay for your long-term care expenses? Don't count on it. Medicare pays for long-term care only under extremely limited circumstances; any other health insurance you may have will not cover long-term care expenses; disability insurance pays benefits only to age 65; and your long-term care insurance may not perform as the salesman promised. You can't count on Medicaid either, because you have to be very poor to receive benefits.

Long-term care costs are so high that they can exhaust your life savings and your children's inheritance. If you don't have sizable savings put away for long-term care and you anticipate the need for such care, purchasing long-term care insurance can be a good idea. The problem is finding a policy that pays the benefits that you think you're buying. You might assume that if you become disabled, you get your benefits. As you will see in Chapter Eleven, it's not that easy.

FOUR

Estate Planning —
The Way It Should Be

By now you realize that there is more than one way to do estate planning. There is the *traditional approach* with a Will and life insurance (i.e., the industry standard), and then there is the better way.

The traditional approach.

You set up a meeting with your estate planning attorney. He gathers the data he needs to prepare your documents:

- The names of the persons you want to receive your property, including any special bequests you wish to make
- If you have minor children, the name(s) of the guardian(s) for your children and sometimes the names of their trustees

In a few days, you meet with your attorney to sign your Will. The process is complete.

As we discussed in the previous chapters, traditional estate planning results in a Will that usually comes with no guarantees that your assets will reach your children or be used for the purposes you intended. It's what your attorney decides for you, not necessarily what you would choose if your were educated about all of the options available to you.

The traditional approach is based on erroneous assumptions and fuzzy thinking. You assume that a Will provides the protection you want for your family. You haven't spelled out the kinds of protection you're looking for and under what circumstances the protection should be provided. You're not even informed of all of the possibilities. Your attorney assumes that he knows what you want to do and that a Will is the right way to get the job done. It's no wonder the process often does not work.

The way it should be — an alternative approach.

The traditional approach is merely guesswork. There is no time devoted to determining precisely what your goals are. And there is no attempt to match your goals to the documents that are prepared for you. The *alternative approach* addresses these shortcomings. The only similarity between the two approaches is that you still contact your attorney and set up an appointment to meet with him. The steps involved in the alternative approach are as follows:

Step 1. Decide what you want your estate plan to do.

Because you probably have never thought about your specific estate planning goals, a *goals checklist*, such as the one that follows, is essential. It lists the most common goals you'll want to consider. You and your spouse check off separately the goals that are important to each of you. You can also add additional goals not found on the checklist. Page 50 offers a sample goals checklist for married couples, and page 52 offers another goals checklist for single persons.

Step 2. Complete a financial questionnaire about your estate.

Your attorney needs to know about the dollar value and types of assets in your estate. Some of the information summarized here includes bank accounts, brokerage accounts, life insurance polices, retirement plans, businesses owned, real estate holdings, etc. Also important is the way your assets are titled (*fee simple, tenants in common*, or joint tenancy with right of survivorship). The information you provide is necessary to select the appropriate strategies needed to meet your goals. Financial questionnaires appear in Appendix B. For easier understanding, the financial questionnaires use the word "separate" to refer to sole ownership, rather than "fee simple."

Step 3. Send the goals checklist and financial data
to your attorney and set an appointment to meet.

Your meeting will be more productive if you send your goals checklist and financial data for review prior to your appointment. Your attorney will have time to think about specific financial data that needs clarification and alternative ways to achieve your goals.

Step 4. Meet with your attorney and finalize a plan.

You can expect to be asked questions about your family members and assets. Your goals checklist will be reviewed with you, and he'll discuss how your goals can be accomplished. You'll be informed of problems you may have overlooked, such as universal life insurance policies that are likely to lapse before your death.

With your input, your attorney will design a plan specifically for you that will accomplish your goals. For larger estates he will want to meet with your financial advisors, such as your CPA and insurance agent, before finalizing the design. The purpose is to get their input, their approval and determine what their role will be in the new plan.

The main purpose is to tailor an estate plan for you rather that give you a generic one size fits all solution. You will be shown how you can complete your estate plan all at once, in stages, or how you can prioritize your goals and choose only those most important to you. To assist

Sample Goals Checklist for Married Couples

YOUR ESTATE PLANNING GOALS

It is important to creat an estate plan for you that meets all of your goals.
Please indicate all goals that are important to you.
Use blank lines to add other goals and comments.
(You have permission to copy and enlarge this sample.)

Husband	Wife	Goals
		Avoid a court-appointed guardianship if one or both of us should become mentally disabled (as from a stroke, head injury, Alzheimer's, etc.)
		Avoid probate and the fees and expenses associated with probate.
		Guarantee that I will control my assets during my lifetime.
		Spend $500 or less for my documents.
		Leave my assets to my loved ones and hope for the best.
		Leave my assets to my loved ones and guarantee that my assets will be protected for them.
		Provide meaningful instructions for the care of my minor children.
		Protect my children from their creditors and their failed marriages.
		Provide incentives for my adult children to live in desired ways.
		Encourage my family members to be financially responsible.
		Prevent my children from having disputes over the assets they inherit.
		Provide for the needs of a disabled child.
		continued on the next page

continued from the previous page

Husband	Wife	Goals
		Guarantee that my assets are passed on to my children, rather than my spouse's children. (Second marriage issue)
		Disinherit a child.
		Provide financially for parents.
		Maintain privacy from outsiders.
		Support the charities of my choice
		Protect my assets from my future creditors.
		Reduce estate taxes.
		Pay no estate taxes (by making charity a partner).
		Keep my children from paying estate taxes at their deaths on assets I give them.
		Find more income to live on by selling appreciated assets.
		After my death, gain income tax benefits for my family by "stretching-out" distributions from my IRA.
		Keep family business, farm or land holding intact for my family after my death.
		Develop a plan to keep my business running smoothly, if I were to die unexpectedly.

Sample Goals Checklist for Single Persons

YOUR ESTATE PLANNING GOALS

It is important to creat an estate plan for you that meets all of your goals.
Please indicate all goals that are important to you.
Use blank lines to add other goals and comments.
(You have permission to copy and enlarge this sample.)

Check	Goals
	Avoid a court-appointed guardianship if I should become mentally disabled (as from a stroke, head injury, Alzheimer's, etc.)
	Avoid probate and the fees and expenses associated with probate.
	Guarantee that I will control my assets during my lifetime.
	Spend $500 or less for my documents.
	Leave my assets to my loved ones and hope for the best.
	Leave my assets to my loved ones and guarantee that my assets will be protected for them.
	Provide meaningful instructions for the care of my minor children.
	Protect my children from their creditors and their failed marriages.
	Provide incentives for my adult children to live in desired ways.
	Prevent my children from having disputes over the assets they inherit.
	Encourage my family members to be financially responsible.
	Provide for the needs of a disabled child.
	Disinherit a child.
	continued on the next page

continued from the previous page

Check	Goals
	Provide financially for parents.
	Maintain privacy from outsiders.
	Support the charities of my choice
	Protect my assets from my future creditors.
	Reduce estate taxes.
	Pay no estate taxes (by making charity a partner).
	Keep my children from paying estate taxes at their deaths on assets I give them (by using generation-skipping tax exemption).
	Find more income to live on by selling appreciated assets.
	After my death, gain income tax benefits for my family by "stretching-out" distributions from my IRA.
	Keep family business, farm or land holding intact for my family after my death.
	Develop a plan to keep my business running smoothly, if I were to die unexpectedly.
	Keep my children from having to support me in my declining years.

you in your decision making, the cost involved to accomplish each of your goals will be spelled out. It is usually best to work with an attorney who will quote, in advance, a flat fee for his work, rather than an attorney who charges by the hour.

If you are working with a conscientious attorney, he will make sure that your assets are properly titled and your beneficiary designations are correct. This is an essential step to make your plan work. The fee for this work is usually quoted separately.

There are no surprises. You know what you'll be getting and how much it will cost. You'll leave the meeting knowing that, when your plan is completed, it will meet your expectations because it has targeted your goals and used strategies that work.

Step 5. Meet to sign your documents.

Review the documents and sign them. Your attorney will tell you of any additional steps that need to be taken.

Step 6. You and your attorney review your plan annually.

At least once a year, your estate planning attorney contacts you to determine if there have been any changes in your major assets or if particular family needs require updates to your original plan. He also amends your documents, if necessary, to conform to changes in the tax laws.

A comparison of the two approaches to estate planning.

The standard form of estate planning practiced today is the traditional approach. Usually clients are the passive recipients of the estate plans benevolently prescribed by their attorneys. Clients get what their attorneys decide for them, which is often not what clients would have wanted had they been educated by their attorneys about estate planning. This is because their attorneys seldom bother to find out what their clients hope to accomplish, and lack the expertise to act on their wishes, even if they were known. Often, the only information requested from clients is the bare essentials necessary to fill in the blanks on standard form documents. What passes for estate planning today, is for the most part just wishful thinking on the part of the client and minimal effort on the part of the attorney.

In contrast, the alternative approach to estate planning is a collaborative process between you and a knowledgeable estate planning attorney. With his help, you define your goals and determine your priorities. This becomes the basis for the estate plan you design together, and the basis for the documents he custom crafts for you.

A Will or a revocable living trust, which is best for you?

Wills and revocable living trusts are the two main documents that attorneys use in basic estate planning. Ideally, you and your attorney should make the choice between these documents based on which one best accomplishes your goals, given the type of assets you own. Unfortunately what often happens today is that an attorney's personal bias determines which of the documents he recommends. Your goals have nothing to do with it.

As you read the following discussion about how well a Will or living trust achieves several common goals, you'll see a definite pattern emerging. A revocable living trust is the superior choice for meeting common goals.

Avoiding Probate.

Wills usually guarantee probate. But assets titled in the name of your living trust completely avoid probate. Furthermore if you have a Will and own real estate in more than one state, you **will** be facing probate in each of those states. Going through probate in one state is hard enough, but having to do it in two states would create unnecessary expense and stress on your family. By titling your assets in the name of your living trust, you can avoid probate in any state, including your own. (Throughout this book "living trust" is used as the shortened form of "revocable living trust.")

Avoiding a court appointed guardianship.

A *fully funded living trust* (one which contains all of your assets) is the best approach for guaranteeing that you are protected from a court-appointed guardianship in case you become mentally disabled and can no longer handle your financial affairs. Upon becoming mentally disabled, your disability trustee (someone you trust, such as your spouse) automatically takes over your finances and takes care of you, your spouse and dependent children. With a fully funded living trust a guardian won't need to be appointed, and your spouse won't have to hire a lawyer to beg the probate court judge for money to pay her living expenses or to buy a pair of shoes. If you have children from a former marriage, your spouse won't have to face challenges in probate court from them, every time she requests money from the court for groceries or other items. With a living trust you plan for the future, well in advance of a mental disability, by choosing the trustee who will disburse your funds according to the written instructions contained in your trust. For example, if you don't want to be placed in a nursing home, then add language to your trust that instructs your trustee to pay for skilled nursing care at home for as long as that is financially feasible.

Guardianships are expensive because fees must be paid to attorneys, the guardian, the insurance bonding company, and the probate court. A physician or psychologist also has to be paid to testify either in court or by deposition about the disabled person's lack of capacity to make significant responsible decisions.

In Chapter 2 George Sanders wanted control over all of his assets. But when he had a stroke his wife Rose didn't have money to pay bills. Rose had to petition the probate court to be appointed George's guardian and obtain the probate court's permission each time she wanted to access his bank and stock brokerage accounts to buy something for herself.

Had George used a fully funded revocable living trust, he would have retained control of his assets. Upon his disability he would have avoided a court appointed guardianship. His assets would have been titled as follows:

George Sanders and Rose Sanders, Trustees, or their successors in trust, under the George Sanders Living Trust, dated June 1, 2002, and any amendments thereto.

Rose as co-trustee of George's revocable living trust would have had immediate and guaranteed access to George's assets. She would have been able to step in and manage George's assets without interference by a financial institution or the probate court. Banks and brokerage companies greet a trustee with open arms because they know that a trustee has absolute power to remove all trust assets and invest them elsewhere.

A Will provides no protection for you and your family if you become mentally disabled because a Will takes effect only at death. Attorneys who favor Wills use durable powers of attorney for disability planning. A durable power of attorney is typically a boilerplate form that gives your spouse or adult child authority to manage your financial affairs while you are living. Most of these documents are effective immediately upon signing, rather than upon an individual's mental incapacity. Durable powers of attorney aren't written with a lot of thought and rarely provide funds for a mentally disabled person's spouse and dependent children. It is easy for someone to commit fraud with a durable power of attorney, because it is just a simple form anyone can prepare and get signed. This is one reason why banks, brokerage companies, and buyers of real estate don't always honor them. These groups prefer to deal with the legal owner, such as the trustee of a living trust, rather than the lowly agent of a durable power of attorney.

Many family squabbles erupt over powers of attorney, both durable and non-durable. Often the elderly are victimized when they knowingly or unknowingly grant a power of attorney to a family member who mishandles their funds. Other family members then rush to file a petition with the probate court to have a guardian appointed from their group, because a guardianship automatically revokes a power of attorney. The probate judge appoints his choice for guardian, often the county attorney, to preserve the assets. Family fights such as these are avoided by using a fully funded revocable living trust.

Maintaining privacy.

Because a Will is a public document, a living trust should be used anytime maintaining privacy is an issue. With a living trust, only you and your trustee need to know, for example, what instructions you are leaving for the care of your minor children, what incentives you are providing for your adult children to live in desired ways, and how you hope to encourage your family members to be financially responsible. If you leave these instructions in a Will, your private concerns and family problems will be open to anyone curious enough to look. A living trust keeps such family concerns away from the prying eyes of the public, and spares family members undue pain and embarrassment.

Guaranteeing that your assets are protected for your loved ones.

If your goal is to guarantee that your assets are protected for your loved ones, your Will is not going to be of any help in protecting your life insurance, the major asset of many families. The proceeds of a life insurance policy pass directly to the person you name as beneficiary. The only way your Will can control the policy proceeds is if you name your "estate" as the beneficiary — something you should not do. In Chapter 2, John's life insurance proceeds were paid directly to his wife, Mary, setting the stage for her and her children to lose them. The situation would not have been any better if John had named his estate as the beneficiary, because that would have made his insurance proceeds part of his probate estate. His creditors would have feasted on the proceeds, leaving Mary only the leftovers that would have been paid outright to her in accordance with the terms of the Will. Insurance proceeds aren't subject to creditors' claims **unless** they are paid into the *decedent's* (the person who died) probate estate. Some attorneys and insurance agents forget this when they name an estate as the alternate beneficiary of a life insurance policy in order to put funds into the children's trusts contained in a Will.

These problems can be avoided by naming your living trust as beneficiary of your life insurance policy, because a living trust protects the insurance proceeds for your family. Upon your death the insurance proceeds will be paid into your living trust, free from the claims of your creditors, and free from probate. Naming your living trust as beneficiary also guarantees that your family won't inadvertently lose the insurance proceeds if you die and your spouse remarries. The trust language can give your spouse almost absolute control over the funds. However, the trust prevents the insurance from ending up in an account that is unintentionally titled in the name of your spouse and her new husband.

If you want to further protect your insurance proceeds and other trust assets, you can also put restrictions on the distribution of trust principal. A restriction sometimes added to a living trust says, "If my spouse survives me and later remarries, pay her the income from my trust, but don't pay her any principal from my trust while she is remarried." Unless your trust says otherwise, *trust income* is composed of interest and dividends, not capital gains.

Controlling your assets during your lifetime.

Keeping control of your assets during your lifetime, while still providing protection should you become mentally disabled, is another one of those goals best accomplished by a living trust. If you recall the story of Mrs. Smith from Chapter 2, she couldn't sell her house and go live with her sister in Phoenix because her home was owned in joint tenancy with right of survivorship with her son and daughter. Mrs. Smith's daughter wouldn't allow her to sell the house because she believed it would be hard to take care of her mother if she moved out of state. All Mrs. Smith wanted to do was to create a plan that would allow her children to take care of her if she became mentally disabled. However, the way she chose to accomplish that goal — owning assets with her children in joint tenancy with right of survivorship — caused her to lose control of her home and stocks. Had Mrs. Smith put her house and stocks in a revocable living trust, she could have named her son and daughter as disability trustees, allowing them to take care of her if she ever became mentally disabled. However, until that time she would have been able to sell her house and move to Phoenix whenever she wanted to, without obtaining her daughter's permission.

Spend $500 or less for your documents.

If your goal is to spend $500 (or less) on your documents, then you are limiting yourself to a Will. Fees for well-written revocable living trusts are in the four digits.

Leaving your assets to your loved ones and hoping for the best.

If your primary goal is to leave everything to your spouse and hope for the best, a *simple Will* (such as the Will in Appendix A) fits the criteria. Simple Wills usually say, "I leave everything to my spouse, if she survives me, and if she does not survive me, then to my children." The problem with a simple Will is that things don't always work out for the best, and when problems or unanticipated complications arise, a simple Will offers no provision for dealing with them. Simple Wills should come marked with a warning label that reads: "WARNING! This document does not protect your family." In Chapter 2, John had a simple Will that didn't protect his family. After John's death his wife and children, in several common scenarios, inadvertently lost a large portion of his life insurance proceeds and other assets.

If you do decide to use a Will, at a minimum don't leave your assets outright to your spouse. (The assets we're talking about are those that your Will controls after giving away specific items such as household effects, car and residence.) Instead, create a Marital Trust in your Will for your spouse's benefit, and leave your assets to your Marital Trust. This at least will guarantee that your spouse won't cause a lot of problems for herself and your children by titling some of your assets in joint tenancy with right of survivorship. In Chapter 2, if Elaine's husband had left the money market account to her in a Marital Trust, she would not have accidentally disinherited her son when she added her daughter's name to the account. However, adding a Marital Trust to John's Will wouldn't have helped protect Mary, because John's Will didn't control the disposition of his major assets.

With a living trust, you need a pour-over Will.

Should you choose a revocable living trust, you still need to have a *pour-over Will*. The Will simply says that, "If I forgot to put some of my assets in my trust, put them in there soon after my death." Your pour-over Will also names the guardian of your minor children.

Some advanced estate planning tools.

Listed below are advanced planning tools that don't come into play if you have a modest size estate. These tools are additional documents that supplement your Will or revocable living trust to accomplish your goals for asset protection (protecting assets from the claims of future creditors) and estate tax savings:

- Irrevocable Life Insurance Trust
- Dynasty Trust
- Qualified Personal Residence Trust
- Family Limited Partnership
- Limited Liability Company
- Charitable Lead Trust
- Charitable Remainder Trust
- Family Foundation

A word to the wise: Advanced planning tools are only as good as the individuals you select to draft and administer them. If a particular document is not properly drafted or administered, then you may never realize the expected tax savings or asset protection. For a simplified explanation of these advanced tools, read Gregory Englund's *Beyond Death & Taxes* (listed in the Suggested Reading section in the back of this book).

Using life insurance to help accomplish your goals.

Because most families are not going to have enough financial resources to accomplish everything for their children that their goals would require, they often purchase life insurance. A frequently asked question is how much insurance to buy. A simple way to find the answer is to write down what your hopes and dreams are for your spouse and children if you aren't here to provide for them. It becomes obvious how much money will be needed. For families with young children $1 million of life insurance should be the minimum amount.

You want your family to be able to live off the income generated from investing the life insurance proceeds. At a six percent return on investment, that means only $60,000 per year from $1 million of insurance proceeds. Once your family starts using the principal, the $1 million will gradually disappear.

In addition to providing cash to your spouse and children, life insurance can be used to accomplish numerous other estate planning goals. For example, life insurance is often purchased to pay estate taxes, so that the family farm or business can remain intact. It is used to equalize an inheritance where your son gets the family business and your daughter receives the insurance proceeds. It can also be used to help your business run smoothly if you were to unexpectedly die. As discussed on page 40, the problem with life insurance is that most people out live their term policy, and many cash value policies do not have guaranteed premiums and guaranteed death benefits. This creates uncertainty as to whether the insurance proceeds will be paid.

Cost considerations.

It usually costs less initially to have a Will prepared than a revocable living trust. However, in addition to monetary costs there are also emotional costs associated with estate planning. As you develop your plan, it is important to factor in both of these costs.

Chapter 3 briefly mentioned the myth that probate is no big deal. Should you decide to do no planning or use a Will and life insurance as your only estate planning tools, then you are guaranteeing that your estate will be supervised by the probate court. A Will guarantees probate. The monetary cost of the probate procedure can be substantial, particularly if you have numerous assets. The monetary cost depends on the attorney picked to do the probate work. In cases where the surviving spouse cannot access accounts to pay household expenses because assets are tied up in the probate process, emotional costs are incurred as well.

Monetary and emotional costs will also arise if you become mentally disabled and have no plan in place that avoids a court-appointed guardianship. You and your family will be dependent on the decisions of a total stranger, the probate judge. Remember, a Will does nothing to avoid a court-appointed guardianship if you become mentally disabled.

The cost of preparing a Will is not a good value if it doesn't meet your goals. The same can be said for a boilerplate living trust prepared by an attorney who is inexperienced or unconcerned with details.

A well-thought-out estate plan replaces wishful thinking with guaranteed outcomes. In addition, a well-drafted plan can more than pay for itself in estate tax savings. It is common to realize estate tax savings equal to 100 times or more the cost of drafting the legal documents. This is a point you will want to consider when finalizing your choice of goals.

The cost of preparing your estate plan will be directly proportional to its complexity — the more elements and the more sophistication, the higher the cost. However, you can usually satisfy multiple goals with the same legal document. Remember, too, that you can usually accomplish your plan in stages, so that the preparation cost is spread over a longer period of time.

Legal fees for estate planning are in keeping with what you would expect to pay for services from other professionals who are specialists in their fields. The lasting value you receive from your estate plan has to be weighed against the cost. Taken in comparison with other family expenditures such as orthodontist fees, cars, vacations, big screen televisions, season sports tickets, summer camp, etc., it is an exceptionally good value!

A word of caution.

With the proliferation of all types of PC software, these days, you may be tempted to draft your own Will and maybe even a revocable living trust, as a cost-saving measure. Unfortunately, although what you might produce is a document that will be legal in your state, the end product will not be equivalent to what you should expect from a legal expert. Without the necessary legal knowledge and expertise, you have no way of gauging the potential pitfalls of your computer-generated documents. You are doing little to protect your family if the documents you produce don't meet your estate planning goals. Remember, that you probably get what you pay for — bare bones boilerplate, which is of minimal utility.

If you are considering a revocable living trust, make sure that an experienced estate planning attorney is advising you. In recent years, hucksters have been peddling living trusts to seniors who don't need them. You should also be wary of sales people who push boilerplate living trusts in an attempt to sell other products such as annuities and life insurance.

Also be wary of estate and income tax savings strategies that are promoted by some marketers of insurance products and the attorneys they work with. You can spend a lot of money investing in a tax savings strategy only to have its highly touted tax benefits denied by the IRS and Congress. A perfect example is the now defunct *charitable split-dollar life insurance program*, which was heavily promoted in the 1990s by several major U.S. insurance companies. Although the strategy did not appear to violate any provision of the Internal Revenue Code, Congress decided it was abusive and wiped out the tax breaks. The thousands of people who had purchased charitable split-dollar policies were left reeling.

FIVE

The Process In Action

Mary and John Revisited.

Let's catch up with Mary and John from Chapter Two. It is three years later. They are now 38 years old, and John is the *sole proprietor* of a successful and growing construction company. Mary is seven months pregnant with their third child. They have outgrown their existing home and plan to purchase a larger $250,000 home for their growing family. They plan to pay $50,000 as a down payment, and obtain a $200,000 mortgage for the balance.

Mary's sister, Suzanne, and her husband recently had their Wills rewritten to provide for their new baby. Suzanne advised Mary to see if she needed to do the same for her expected child. Mary looked at her Will and saw that it did not include any provision for a third child. The real estate lawyer who prepared Mary and John's Wills had not planned for this event and did not include the necessary language. A year after he wrote their Wills, the real estate lawyer retired and moved to Florida. John's CPA referred them to an estate planning attorney. Mary and John want to protect their family.

John called the attorney to set up an appointment. The attorney faxed John a financial questionnaire and goals checklist to be completed and returned, prior to the appointment. A blank goals checklist is set out in Chapter 4, page 50, and a blank financial questionnaire for a married couple is in Appendix B.

Their Goals.

A copy of Mary and John's completed goals checklist appears on page 68. They both have the same goals:

- Avoid a court appointed guardianship if one (or both of us) should become mentally disabled, as from a stroke, head injury, Alzheimer's, etc.

- Avoid probate and the fees and expenses associated with probate

- Leave my assets to my loved ones, and guarantee that my assets will be protected for them

- Provide meaningful instructions for the care of my minor children

- Protect my children from their creditors and their failed marriages

- Protect my assets from my future creditors

- Reduce estate taxes

Their Financial Snapshot.

Mary and John have a joint checking account with a balance of $2,000. They have a $20,000 joint money market account. Their current house is titled as joint tenants with right of survivorship. They plan to title their new home in Mary's name, because they believe that the nature of John's business makes him vulnerable to lawsuits.

John rolled over his 401(k) assets to an IRA when he quit his job to start his own business. The IRA is currently worth $35,000. John still has the $250,000 term life insurance policy that names Mary the primary beneficiary and his children as the contingent beneficiaries. His IRA has the same beneficiary designations.

Mary and John also have a brokerage account, titled as joint tenants with right of survivorship. The current market value of the account is $15,000.

John's construction company builds and finishes office interiors for tenants of large office buildings. The business is not incorporated. John estimates that his net income this year will be $100,000, and that the business is worth $200,000.

The delusion of the traditional approach.

Chances are had Mary and John consulted most attorneys, they would have wound up with the same plan — have Wills prepared, purchase more insurance, and incorporate John's business. Their Wills would look similar to the one in Appendix A, and would accomplish only two of the goals on the goals checklist:

- Spend $500 or less for my documents
- Leave my assets to my loved ones and hope for the best

After signing their Wills, they would have left their attorney's office feeling like they had done something wonderful for their children. In reality, Mary and John's Wills would have accomplished little more than naming their children's guardian. As we have previously discussed in Chapter 2, all sorts of bad things can happen to good people, and in this instance, bad things would end up thwarting Mary and John's wishes. Their Wills, essentially, would leave everything to fate. This is not what Mary and John would have chosen if they had known about what can go wrong.

Mary and John's Goals Checklist

YOUR ESTATE PLANNING GOALS

It is important to creat an estate plan for you that meets all of your goals.
Please indicate all goals that are important to you.
Use blank lines to add other goals and comments.

Husband	Wife	Goals
X	X	Avoid a court-appointed guardianship if one or both of us should become mentally disabled (as from a stroke, head injury, Alzheimer's, etc.)
X	X	Avoid probate and the fees and expenses associated with probate.
		Guarantee that I will control my assets during my lifetime.
		Spend $500 or less for my documents.
		Leave my assets to my loved ones and hope for the best.
X	X	Leave my assets to my loved ones and guarantee that my assets will be protected for them.
X	X	Provide meaningful instructions for the care of my minor children.
X	X	Protect my children from their creditors and their failed marriages.
		Provide incentives for my adult children to live in desired ways.
		Prevent my children from having disputes over the assets they inherit.
		Encourage my family members to be financially responsible.
		Provide for the needs of a disabled child.
		continued on the next page

continued from the previous page

Husband	Wife	Goals
		Disinherit a child.
		Provide financially for parents.
		Maintain privacy from outsiders.
		Support the charities of my choice
X	X	Protect my assets from my future creditors.
X	X	Reduce estate taxes.
		Pay no estate taxes (by making charity a partner).
		Keep my children from paying estate taxes at their deaths on assets I give them (by using generation-skipping tax exemption).
		Find more income to live on by selling appreciated assets.
		After my death, gain income tax benefits for my family by "stretching-out" distributions from my IRA.
		Keep family business, farm or land holding intact for my family after my death.
		Develop a plan to keep my business running smoothly, if I were to die unexpectedly.

A Plan for Mary and John.

Although they are young and have limited assets, Mary and John want an estate plan that will take care of them, their children, and John's business. They are looking for something that's not complicated. They are on a budget and are willing to build their plan in stages, over time.

Their estate planning attorney wants to design a plan that will meet the goals Mary and John selected on their goals checklist. The plan needs a firm foundation. The cornerstones of the foundation will be two revocable living trusts, one for Mary and one for John. These revocable living trusts, if properly drafted, will satisfy all of their goals, except protecting their assets from creditors. Revocable living trusts do not protect assets from the claims of the trust maker's creditors. However, Mary and John's separate living trusts hopefully will prevent the creditors of one spouse from seizing the assets of both. Chapter Six contains a detailed explanation of how John's revocable living trust works.

John's construction business, which is currently a *sole proprietorship* (which means that John is doing business in his own name as an individual), exposes him to serious risk from lawsuits. As a sole proprietor John is personally liable for all claims against his business. To hold down attorney's fees, Mary and John decide that at this time to only protect their personal assets from the claims of John's business creditors. The *asset protection planning* they decide upon is discussed in Chapter Nine. In the future they can add to their estate plan if and when additional needs arise, for example, to protect their personal assets from the claims of their personal creditors, to further reduce estate taxes, or to keep their business in the family.

Prepare pour-over wills for Mary & John.

Mary and John's revocable living trusts don't eliminate their need for Wills. They each need what's called a *pour-over Will* which in effect says, "If I forgot to put something in my living trust, put it in there upon my death." Mary and John also need the pour-over Wills to name Mary's sister, Suzanne, as the guardian of their minor children.

Transferring assets into Mary and John's revocable living trusts.

Immediately upon completing Mary and John's revocable living trusts, their attorney begins the process of transferring their assets to their living trusts. This is the key element in living trust planning, because each trust can control only those assets that are titled in the trust's name. This process of transferring assets to the revocable trusts is called *funding*.

Purchasing additional insurance.

An essential element of the plan to protect their children is for Mary and John to have sufficient life insurance. How much life insurance do they need? They can easily determine this for themselves by writing down instructions for the care of their minor children. (See Appendix C.) All Mary and John have to do now is to estimate the cost of each of the instructions and total up the amounts.

In addition, John should make sure that his life insurance is sufficient to take care of the more common situation where Mary and the kids survive him. The insurance will be needed to replace his lost income at least until his children have completed college. Although Mary doesn't have any life insurance, she should buy some to protect her husband and children. If Mary dies, leaving John to raise their minor children, John will need to hire a full time nanny/housekeeper. He will not be able to run his construction business and raise three young children without considerable help.

John should also purchase disability insurance that will protect him until age 65. His family will need the income to pay for living expenses in the event John becomes disabled. The main feature of a disability policy is the definition of "total disability." John should make sure that his disability policy pays benefits if "because of injury or sickness he is unable to perform the important duties of his occupation."

The net result.

All of Mary and John's goals are met with the living trust plan described in Chapter Six and the asset protection plan for John's business described in Chapter Nine. Mary and John now have an estate plan that offers more than the illusion of protection for them and their family. They've got the real thing: a well-designed plan, complete with guarantees.

SIX

Anatomy of a Living Trust

Mary and John's attorney chooses separate revocable living trusts for each of them. Because their goals are identical, the provisions for both trusts are nearly the same. Their attorney selects John's trust as an example to explain how each trust works.

John's living trust is pictured on page75. Mary and John are co-trustees of John's living trust. It can be visualized as a four-drawer file cabinet. When a major life event happens (e.g., John's death), the trustee opens up a particular drawer and reads the instructions that are stored there.

THE TOP DRAWER

The top drawer is the only drawer that is opened while John is alive.

Contents of the Top Drawer.

John's top drawer is empty until he funds his living trust. The funding process, which begins immediately after the trust is created, is discussed in Chapter Seven. While John is alive all assets transferred to his trust automatically end up in the top drawer.

John's living trust will be named as the beneficiary of his life insurance policy. If the insurance is in force at his death, the proceeds will be paid into the top drawer of his trust.

Other assets that will be transferred to John's trust at the time of its creation are:

- $15,000 brokerage account currently owned by John and Mary

- Membership interest certificates for the limited liability company formed to operate John's construction company (see Chapter Nine)

- Household and personal effects

Upon John's death his household and personal effects are distributed directly to Mary. John's trust can also provide for specific distributions of cash and property at his death to family members, friends and, charities. Couples sometimes write their trusts so that specific distributions (e.g., $1,000 to each favorite niece and nephew) are paid from the trust of the second spouse to die.

The Top Drawer Avoids a Court-Appointed
Guardianship and Probate.

By placing most of his assets in the top drawer of his trust, John avoids a court- appointed guardianship, should he become mentally disabled. The definition of mental disability is contained in the trust, and is not determined by a court. For example, the trust can state that John is mentally disabled only if a committee made up of his treating physician, wife and brother all agree in writing to that fact. Mary, as co-trustee of John's living trust, doesn't have to go to the probate court

THE JOHN HARDY LIVING TRUST

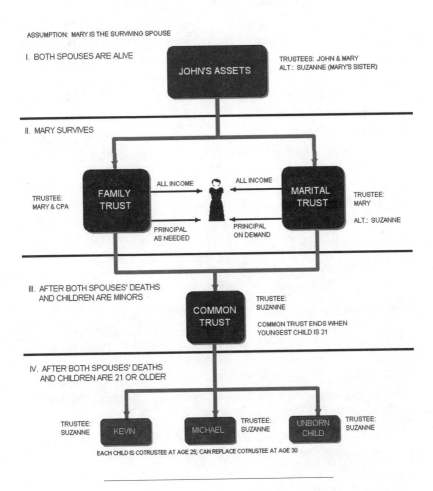

ASSUMPTION: MARY IS THE SURVIVING SPOUSE

I. BOTH SPOUSES ARE ALIVE

JOHN'S ASSETS

TRUSTEES: JOHN & MARY
ALT.: SUZANNE (MARY'S SISTER)

II. MARY SURVIVES

TRUSTEE:
MARY & CPA

FAMILY TRUST

ALL INCOME →

ALL INCOME ←

MARITAL TRUST

TRUSTEE:
MARY

ALT.: SUZANNE

PRINCIPAL
AS NEEDED →

PRINCIPAL
ON DEMAND ←

III. AFTER BOTH SPOUSES' DEATHS
AND CHILDREN ARE MINORS

COMMON TRUST

TRUSTEE:
SUZANNE

COMMON TRUST ENDS WHEN
YOUNGEST CHILD IS 21

IV. AFTER BOTH SPOUSES' DEATHS
AND CHILDREN ARE 21 OR OLDER

TRUSTEE:
SUZANNE

KEVIN

MICHAEL

TRUSTEE:
SUZANNE

UNBORN CHILD

TRUSTEE:
SUZANNE

EACH CHILD IS COTRUSTEE AT AGE 25; CAN REPLACE COTRUSTEE AT AGE 30

to be appointed John's guardian, because she already has immediate access to and control over his trust assets. Also, should John pass away, the living trust guarantees that his trust assets will avoid the cost and anxiety associated with probate.

THE SECOND DRAWER

Soon after John's death, still assuming he dies before Mary, John's attorney transfers the assets remaining in the top drawer of his living trust to the second drawer, where he places them in one or both of the following two files:

- The *Family Trust* (often called *the unified credit trust, bypass trust* or *Trust B*)
- The *Marital Trust* (often called the marital deduction trust or *Trust A*)

The top drawer is never opened again, and while Mary is the surviving spouse the second drawer is the only drawer that is open. Upon John's death he can no longer revoke or amend his trust, and consequently the trust automatically becomes irrevocable.

Contents of the Second Drawer.

The assets that will end up in the second drawer are as follows:

- The assets remaining in the top drawer after distribution of his personal and household effects, and payment of specific distributions, debts, attorney's fees and funeral expenses
- Assets titled in John's name which are poured-over at death by his Will to his living trust
- Proceeds of John's life insurance policy as a result of naming his trust as beneficiary

Recall that Mary is the primary beneficiary of John's IRA. If Mary survives John, the IRA proceeds will not pass through John's living trust. Instead Mary becomes the beneficiary of John's IRA. Mary can either remain the beneficiary or she can elect to "roll over" John's IRA to her IRA. If she does not have an IRA, she can set one up at that time. Because the wrong choice can generate additional estate and income taxes, a surviving spouse in this situation should seek the advice of the attorney who wrote the original plan or a CPA who is knowledgeable about IRA distribution rules, before "rolling over" her deceased husband's IRA.

Purpose of the Second Drawer.

The purpose of the second drawer is to save taxes on the assets of the first spouse to die, and to protect those assets for the surviving spouse and children. The Family Trust and the Marital Trust can be written to give Mary, as trust beneficiary, almost outright ownership of the assets they contain. However, both of these trusts prevent John's assets from inadvertently going to a new spouse, if Mary were to remarry after John's death. If Mary later remarries, her new husband cannot get to these assets unless Mary intentionally takes the assets out of the second drawer and gives them to him. John is comfortable in knowing that Mary cannot inadvertently lose his assets, and believes this is sufficient protection for his children. If John wants even greater control in preventing his assets from going to a new spouse should Mary remarry, he can place further restrictions on the Family Trust and the Marital Trust so that no trust principal can be withdrawn (only trust income), during the time Mary remains remarried.

The second drawer's Family Trust and Marital Trust also allow John and Mary to maximize their estate tax savings by using both of their $1 million coupons. Everyone is born with a "coupon" that excludes $1 million of his assets from the estate tax. This exclusion, technically called the *applicable exclusion amount,* will rise to $3.5 million in 2009, but will fall back to $1 million in 2011. A married couple, however, doesn't automatically get to pass $2 million to their children without paying an estate tax. The catch for a married couple is that, to use the $1 million coupon of the first spouse to die, that spouse must have a Family Trust (unified credit trust) included in his Will or revocable living trust. In order to receive the full benefit of each spouse's $1 million coupon, assets equaling the coupon amount must be titled either in the name of the first spouse to die or in the name of that spouse's revocable living trust. (If reading about taxes makes your eyes glaze over, you may want to fast forward to "The Third Drawer" on page 83.)

Estate Tax 101.

The details of the federal estate tax are unknown to most people, including tax professionals. Few of us are going to spend any time learning the ins and outs of a tax that applies to less than 2% of the U.S. population. You're probably thinking it doesn't apply to you, but it might. What you may not know about the estate tax is that it applies to everything you own at the time of your death, and even some assets you don't own!

What you own at the time of your death can include your:

- House
- Car
- Household possessions
- Jewelry
- Stocks
- Bank accounts
- Proceeds of life insurance policies you own
- IRAs
- 401(k)
- Annuities, etc.

What you own can also include things that you only have the right to enjoy, such as a vacation home that you deeded to your children but kept the right to live in during your lifetime. The value of these assets can add up fast, especially if you have a million dollar life insurance policy.

The IRS even imposes the estate tax on gifts you made over the years to individuals other than your spouse. A lot of us know that you can give away $11,000 (cash or other assets) per year to as many people as you wish without paying a *gift tax*. The $11,000 amount is called the *annual gift tax exclusion*.

Being the kind-hearted soul that you are, you may have given away more than $11,000 in a single year to someone other than your spouse. Surprise, there's something you weren't told: gifts in a single year that exceed $11,000 (in some cases $22,000, if you're married) are subject to the estate tax at the time of your death. The sum of all these gifts that each year exceed $11,000 (in some cases $22,000) is called your *adjusted taxable gifts*.

But the IRS is not entirely without a heart. After you total all of the assets you own at the time of your death, and all of those other assets that the IRS claims they can tax, you get some deductions, including:

- Your mortgage
- Your other debts
- Funeral expenses
- Attorney fees
- Executor fees
- Any charitable bequests

But that's not all! Married couples get to delay paying estate taxes. The first spouse to die gets a deduction for all property left to his/her spouse. It's called the *marital deduction*. Because of the marital deduction, a married man with a $10 million dollar estate can completely avoid the estate tax with a one sentence Will that says, "I leave all my property to my beloved wife, Samantha." However, when Samantha passes on, her estate has all the couple's assets, and all the tax problems that go along with them.

The estate tax is computed by using a tax table that comes from the Internal Revenue Code. In 2003 the highest tax rate was 49% and will decline to 45% in 2007. You are taxed on the sum of your *taxable estate* (everything the IRS says you own, minus the deductions) and your adjusted taxable gifts. Any gift tax that should have paid in the past is subtracted. The amount you end up with is called the gross estate tax.

When do you get to use your $1 million coupon (i.e., the applicable exclusion amount mentioned in the previous section)? In actuality you don't deduct $1 million from your estate taxes. Instead you get a credit that reduces the gross estate tax. This credit is called the *unified credit* (also known as the *applicable credit amount*). The unified credit in 2003 was $345,800, which is the amount of estate tax that would be due on $1 million of assets.

Using the unified credit and the marital deduction to maximize estate tax savings for a married couple.

There are countless tax journal articles and books that discuss the Family Trust, the Marital Trust and the various ways to divide assets between them to maximize the estate tax savings offered by the unified credit. Maximizing the unified credit (the estate tax savings you get by using your coupon) has always been a difficult topic for lawyers to explain. The first thing many estate planning lawyers discuss with their clients is the tax aspects of the Family Trust and the Marital Trust. The clients usually fall into a stupor, and at the meeting's conclusion, they leave the lawyer's office wondering what he was talking about.

Let's return to the example of the man (let's call George) who left his $10 million estate to his wife, Samantha. George used the marital deduction to completely avoid the estate tax on his death. But he over did it, because he failed to use his $1 million coupon. Upon his death, he could have used his coupon to carve out a $1 million portion of his estate and left the rest to his wife, and still paid no estate tax. The container that would hold this the $1 million portion is called the Family Trust (often called the bypass trust, unified credit trust or Trust B.) The remaining $9 million of George's estate would go to Samantha either outright or in another box called the Marital Trust.

After George's death, Samantha will be able to use all the assets in both the Marital Trust and the Family Trust set up by George's Will (or revocable living trust), as well as all of her own assets. When Samantha dies, her *gross estate* (her total assets subject to the federal estate tax) will contain not only her own assets, but also those in the Marital Trust. The assets in the Family Trust will not be included in Samantha's gross estate if the Family Trust contains the following magic words required by the IRS: "payments of principal are limited to health, education, support or maintenance." At Samantha's death her $1 million coupon will be used automatically to reduce the estate taxes imposed on her taxable estate by $345,800 (in 2003). Her estate won't owe any estate taxes on the assets in the Family Trust, no matter how large those assets have grown.

Estate tax planning for Mary and John.

When the second drawer is opened, there are two main approaches for dividing assets between the Family Trust and the Marital Trust. The first approach is to put assets equal to the coupon of the first spouse to die into the Family Trust, with any excess passing to the Marital Trust. Usually this is accomplished by means of a formula (or alternatively, a specific dollar amount) written into the revocable living trust. This type of plan works well for a married couple whose assets exceed the coupon amount, because it guarantees that each spouse's coupon will be used.

The second approach, which is the one we use for Mary and John, directs all of John's assets to the Marital Trust, when the second drawer is opened. At John's death it becomes Mary's responsibility (assuming she is the surviving spouse) to decide what percentage of John's assets, if any, should be put into the Family Trust. This plan works well for couples such as Mary and John who currently don't have enough assets to be subject to the estate tax.

Mary and John will likely avoid estate taxes without needing to use John's coupon. Their combined taxable estates total approximately $570,000, so there is no need for John's revocable living trust to direct any of his assets to the Family Trust. Instead, John's assets will be placed in the Marital Trust, except for assets that Mary disclaims.

A *disclaimer* is the legal way of saying, "No Thanks." The purpose of the disclaimer is to allow Mary to decide, after John's death, if there is a tax benefit in placing any of John's assets in the Family Trust.

Why does John even need a Family Trust? Mary and John need flexibility for estate tax planning. Although their combined taxable estates are currently well under the coupon amount ($1 million in 2003), it wouldn't take much for them to exceed it. For example, John's

$250,000 life insurance policy is not enough to protect his family. Purchasing an additional $750,000 of life insurance (bringing the total life insurance to $1 million) could subject his family to the estate tax. And if John's business is successful and increases in value, there'll be even more property subject to estate tax. At John's death, Mary can decide if all or a part of John's coupon will be used by disclaiming a percentage of John's assets. The disclaimed assets will go into the Family Trust that exists for the purpose saving estate taxes.

Why not just use the first approach and at John's death fill the Family Trust with John's assets up to the coupon amount and put any excess in the Marital Trust? The reason is that there are additional administrative hassles and costs associated with maintaining the Family Trust. It's not worth the bother unless the Family Trust is needed to reduce estate taxes.

Out with the estate tax, and in with additional income tax.

The 2001 Tax Act repeals the estate tax for the year 2010 only. But wealthy families who inherit assets in 2010 may have to ante up additional income taxes. For 2010 there is a change in the calculation of income taxes on the sale of inherited property, eliminating the current generous income tax break.

Under the current income tax law, an asset sold soon after you inherit it will generally not incur any income taxes. This is because the income tax due is computed on the difference between the selling price and the fair market value of the asset on the day the decedent died. Under the new law in 2010, the income tax is computed on the difference between the selling price and what the decedent originally paid for the asset. Because it will be difficult to prove what the decedent paid for the asset, the IRS will want you to use $0 as the cost, and, for all practical purposes, the entire selling price will be income. Usually this income will be taxed at a lower income tax rate, called the *capital gains rate*. This new income tax law that becomes effective in 2010 doesn't apply to the first $1.3 million of inherited assets. This new income tax law also doesn't apply to an additional $3 million of assets left to a surviving spouse.

THE THIRD DRAWER

After Mary dies, assets remaining in the second drawer of John's living trust (i.e., the assets remaining in the Family Trust and the Marital Trust) move to the third drawer. The third drawer contains only one file, the Common Trust. This is where John gives instructions to his children's guardian and the trustees on how to raise his children. He wants to provide instructions on how the children should be raised in the event he and Mary die while their children are minors. All the details about schools, religious upbringing, music lessons, sports, visits with grandparents, etc., are set forth for the guardian and the trustees of their children. Because John wants to keep these instructions a private affair, they are contained in his living trust. Appendix C contains instructions John includes in his revocable living trust for the care of his minor children.

John chooses to have his living trust written so that the assets remain in the Common Trust until his youngest child reaches age 21, at which time the Common Trust terminates. (John can instead choose to include language that will terminate the Common Trust at a different time, such as when his youngest child "attains age 23 or completes college, whichever is earlier.") John wants his sister-in-law to be the initial trustee. The instructions in the Common Trust will give her a good idea on how to spend the funds for the children while they are growing up.

The main purpose of the third drawer is to make sure that each child has had a chance to complete college before the trust assets are equally divided among them. The third drawer prevents a situation that could arise if Mary and John were to die soon after their oldest child completes college. A lot of the family's money would have been used for their oldest child's college education. In such a case it would not be fair to equally divide the remaining assets among all the children immediately upon the deaths of Mary and John. The children who had not yet attended college would be severely shortchanged. So to be fair to all the children, the trust assets remain in the Common Trust and are spent on all the children's needs, particularly educational needs, until the youngest child's 21st birthday.

THE FOURTH DRAWER

Once John's youngest child reaches the age of 21, the Common Trust terminates and the assets are moved to the fourth drawer. This drawer contains separate files, called children's trusts, one for each of John's children. With John's help each child's trust is designed with the following provisions:

- Income and principal will be paid to or for the benefit of each child from his trust in the sole discretion of the trustee.
- Each child's trust will always have an independent trustee.
- Each child can become a co-trustee of his trust at age 25.
- When a child becomes 30, the child has the right to remove the co-trustee. The co-trustee, however, is not allowed to resign until a CPA, attorney or other independent person has been appointed as the replacement co-trustee.

In John's plan he is leaving his assets to his children in trust for life. The trusts are irrevocable. However, each child's ownership is close to outright ownership, because at age 25 the child becomes a co-trustee of his own separate trust. And at age 30 the child has the right to remove his co-trustee and appoint a replacement co-trustee.

These children's trusts meet John's goal of protecting each child's inheritance from being lost to a child's divorce or to most other creditors of the child. In almost every state the assets of a discretionary trust (i.e., a trust where income and principal are paid at the discretion of the trustee) are not reachable by the beneficiary's creditors as long as

- the trust contains a spendthrift clause , i.e., a clause that states that the trust's assets are not subject to the claims of any creditor
- the beneficiary is neither the trust maker nor the trustee

Consequently, if a child is serving as co-trustee of his own trust and is then sued, the child can just drop out as co-trustee, leaving the remaining trustee to serve alone. The child is in effect telling the creditor,

"I know that a creditor who has a judgment against me can access my trust assets in satisfaction of that judgment if I am both a beneficiary and a co-trustee, but I'm no longer a co-trustee. I'm just a beneficiary, so leave me alone."

As you probably would expect, a child's trust is not going to be much of a roadblock to the IRS. The Internal Revenue Code (Section 6321) and several federal court cases give the IRS ample authority to obtain trust assets in order to satisfy a beneficiary's unpaid income tax bill.

SEVEN

Funding Mary and John's Revocable Living Trusts

Mary and John's living trusts will not avoid probate or a court appointed guardianship unless they are funded, i.e., filled up with assets. It is at this stage of the planning that a lot of attorneys drop the ball and fail to fund the trusts. Don't let this happen to you. Make sure your trust gets funded soon after you sign it.

As Mary and John's attorney funds their trusts he keeps in mind two of their goals:

- Reducing estate taxes
- Protecting assets from claims of future creditors

Right now Mary and John don't have enough assets to be subject to the estate tax, but they may one day. The first estate tax saving strategy is to place half the assets in John's trust and the other half in Mary's. This will maximize their estate tax savings regardless of which spouse dies first. For a complete explanation see Estate Taxes 101, on page78.

There is another reason for wanting to divide Mary and John's assets into separate revocable living trusts. The most basic idea of asset protection planning is for Mary and John to own their assets separately, as in separate revocable living trusts. If Mary and John title their assets as joint tenants with right of survivorship, or lump all their assets together in one joint living trust, they make it that much easier for the creditors of one spouse to seize the assets of both.

Can John just title all his assets in Mary's name and think he has protected his assets from his creditors? Hardly. A judge would take a dim view of this and rule that Mary was just holding John's assets in her name. John's creditors would then be allowed to seize Mary's assets to satisfy John's debts. Consequently John can't be a pig about titling all or most of his assets in Mary's name or in the name of Mary's revocable living trust.

The funding process is accomplished by changing the name on financial accounts, deeds and other assets to the legal name of the trust. The complete legal name of John's trust is as follows:

JOHN HARDY and MARY HARDY, Trustees, or their successors in trust, under the JOHN HARDY LIVING TRUST, dated March 15, 2003, and any amendments thereto.

John's bank and brokerage company will want to use a shorter name, and that's O.K. as long as the name includes at least one trustee, the date of the trust, and a reference that the assets are held by a trustee. The following trust name is perfectly acceptable:

JOHN HARDY and MARY HARDY, Trustees, under the JOHN HARDY LIVING TRUST, dated 3-15-03.

Mary and John's attorney wants to make the funding process as simple as possible. He looks at each asset individually and decides which assets are going to be put in one of the trusts, and which assets are going to be kept outside of the trusts.

Mary and John will each sign an *assignment agreement* to transfer their personal and household effects (e.g., jewelry, furniture and clothes) to their trusts. Upon the death of the first spouse, these assets will transfer immediately to the surviving spouse in accordance with the directions in each of their trusts.

The joint checking account, with a $2,000 balance, will be left alone. Mary and John pay their monthly bills out of this account. It's likely that this account will never be a large sum, and, for convenience, they will continue to hold the account jointly. That way, they won't have to change anything about the checking account they regularly use to pay their bills.

The $20,000 money market account will be transferred to Mary's trust.

Most of it will be used for the down payment on her new home. Mary's parents gave her the $20,000 to help with the down payment and the move.

The $15,000 brokerage account will be transferred to John's trust. Thus each of the revocable living trusts will own some of the couple's liquid assets.

Their attorney will prepare a beneficiary designation for John's $35,000 IRA, which names Mary as the primary beneficiary and John's revocable living trust as the alternate beneficiary. There are detailed rules, set by the IRS, on how to name a revocable trust as the beneficiary of an IRA. Experienced attorneys who work in this area will know the appropriate steps to take. The benefit of naming John's trust as the alternate beneficiary of the IRA is that if he and Mary were to die in a common accident, distributions can be made from the IRA to their minor children without the probate court ever being involved.

Mary and John's new house will be titled in the name of Mary's revocable living trust, at the time of the purchase. The house will be titled in Mary's trust to hopefully prevent John's future creditors, if any, from seizing the house.

Initially, the membership interest certificates of John's construction company, which is being set up as a limited liability company, will be put into his living trust. Some couples choose to split the ownership interests of the family business between the husband and wife's trusts. But in this instance John wanted the construction company to be owned by his living trust and Mary didn't object.

Notice that Mary and John's assets, with the exception of John's business, are being divided evenly between the two trusts. Mary and

John are not attempting to shield assets from John's future creditors by titling everything in Mary's name.

The most important function of Mary and John's revocable living trusts is to act as beneficiaries of their biggest assets — their life insurance policies. Revocable living trusts guarantee that, if Mary and John have untimely deaths, their life insurance proceeds will be held in trust for their minor children, free from claims of creditors and distributed in accordance with their detailed instructions. John should name his living trust as the primary beneficiary of his life insurance policy, and Mary should likewise name her living trust as the primary beneficiary of any life insurance policy she may own in the future. This completes the funding of their trusts.

EIGHT

More Planning Considerations

What's wrong with the way most people name the beneficiary of their life insurance? How does living trust planning differ in a community property state? This chapter explains the answers to these two questions.

Naming beneficiaries of life insurance policies.

It's usually over in little more than a blink of an eye. Your insurance agent asks you whom you want to name as beneficiaries of your life insurance policy, and he writes the names on the appropriate lines. It's hard to believe that something handled so nonchalantly is actually of major importance to your estate plan.

Life insurance policies are contracts. The insurance proceeds will be paid to whomever the policy designates as the beneficiary. The initial beneficiary designation can be found in the insurance policy application attached at the end of the insurance policy. Wills have no control over who receives the insurance proceeds, unless the estate is named as the life insurance beneficiary.

It is critical to choose your beneficiaries carefully. Improper beneficiary designations are a major planning error that sometimes cause unexpected and disastrous results. It is common practice among life insurance professionals, where minor children are involved, to name the surviving spouse as the primary beneficiary of a life insurance policy, and the minor children as the alternate beneficiaries. In most states minors are children under the age of 18.

When parents buy an insurance policy that names their minor children as alternate beneficiaries, they think that if they both were to die the proceeds would go to their minor children, and everything will work out fine. What actually happens is that the insurance proceeds go to the probate court, and the children's guardian cannot touch the principal without the probate judge's written permission. In fact, in busy metropolitan areas, the guardian can't even talk to the judge; but must instead hire an attorney to file a petition requesting funds to care for the children. So parents are in effect telling their minor children, "Kids, if something were to happen to us, we are going to leave your financial well-being to a complete stranger, the probate court judge, and we are not going to give him any instructions on how to take care of you. And when you are eighteen, the judge will give you all the money to spend as you please."

Most lawyers have never considered this problem. Other lawyers in an attempt to correct it, will recommend that the alternate beneficiary of the husband's insurance policy be changed from the minor children to the husband's "Estate." Designating the husband's estate as the alternate beneficiary brings the insurance proceeds into the deceased husband's probate estate. The lawyer's idea is that, if the husband and wife were to die in a common accident, the husband's life insurance proceeds would fill up the children's trusts that are contained in the husband's Will. This strategy is a serious error in judgment on the part of the lawyer, because it allows insurance proceeds to be subject to the claims of the husband's creditors. State law protects life insurance proceeds from the claims of the husband's creditors, unless you make this one colossal mistake and name the estate as the beneficiary of the insurance policy.

John's attorney solves the beneficiary designation problem by naming John's living trust as the beneficiary of John's life insurance. The primary beneficiary is changed to "the Trustees, or successor Trustees, under the John Hardy Living Trust, dated March 15, 2003." Now, if John has an untimely death, the life insurance proceeds go directly to his living trust, rather than to John's probate estate. The proceeds remain free from the claims of his creditors. The trust also packs a powerful punch because it:

- Guarantees that Mary will not inadvertently lose the insurance money
- Guarantees that upon Mary's death the remaining money will get to his children and be protected for them
- Provides meaningful instructions for the care of his minor children

Living trust planning in a community property state.

For married couples there are two different types of property law in the United States. Eight states (i.e., Louisiana, Texas, New Mexico, Arizona, Nevada, California, Washington, and Idaho) base their concept of property ownership, as to husband and wife, on French or Spanish *civil law*. These states and Wisconsin who enacted a marital property law system in 1986 are called the community property states. The other 41 states base their concept of property ownership on English *common law*, and are called the common law property states.

In the community property states all assets acquired during a marriage — except gifts, inheritances and personal injury recoveries — are presumed to be owned half by the husband and half by the wife. If a husband and wife don't want a particular asset to be community property then they can sign a document with the same formalities as a deed declaring the asset to be *separate property*. Each of the nine states has different rules for creating separate property.

Had Mary and John lived in a community property state other than Louisiana, their attorney would have chosen a *joint revocable living trust*, rather than two separate living trusts. A joint living trust works perfectly in a community property state because by operation of law all assets (other than separate property) are owned half by the husband and half by the wife. When the first spouse dies his separate property and half of the community property are directed usually to the Family Trust and a Marital Trust. At the time of the first spouse's death, the surviving spouse transfers her separate property and half of the community property to a subtrust that she controls.

In Louisiana, revocable living trusts are not common. One reason for this is that the basic system of law in Louisiana is French civil law where there is no tradition for trusts. Although the Louisiana Trust Code authorizes the use of trusts, Louisiana has developed some peculiar issues regarding trusts that other states don't have. For example, a *power of appointment* (a trust provision that allows a spouse or child to decide where trust assets go long after the trust maker dies) is not permitted in Louisiana. In the other 49 states a power of appointment is an extremely useful tool that gives a trust a lot of flexibility.

The big problem with community property is that a creditor of one spouse can often reach the entire community property to satisfy a claim. If a couple in a community property state wants to protect their assets from creditors they usually have to begin by creating separate property. They can then use the same asset protection tools as everyone else in the United States. A benefit given up by creating separate property is a special income tax break given to community property when the first spouse dies. This tax break usually allows the surviving spouse to sell both halves of the community property soon after the death of the first spouse without incurring any income tax. In the common law states this tax break (known as the *step-up in basis rule*) also applies to the assets of the first spouse to die, but it does not apply to the surviving spouse's assets until after her death.

NINE

Protecting Assets from Claims of Future Creditors

Mary and John are now ready to focus on a plan to protect their assets from the claims of future creditors. John's construction business is a sole proprietorship (i.e., he is doing business in his own name as an individual). This exposes John's assets and any assets he may own jointly with Mary to serious risk from lawsuits that can arise from John's business dealings.

What is asset protection planning?

Asset protection planning is about legally organizing Mary and John's assets to safeguard them from claims of future creditors. In almost every state, to the extent that Mary and John can get to their assets, so can their creditors. This means that if John creates a revocable or *irrevocable trust* and names himself as the beneficiary, the trust assets will rarely be protected from his creditors. (Alaska, Nevada, Utah, Delaware and Rhode Island are trying to change this by allowing residents and nonresidents to set up asset protection trusts for themselves, in an attempt to attract more cash and hopefully more business to their states.)

Two types of creditors.

There are two types of creditors: inside and outside. *Inside creditors* have claims against John's assets because he directly does business with them. They are creditors of his business. They are his customers and suppliers. John's inside creditors include the companies that sell him his building supplies, lease him his trucks, his accountant, etc.

Outside creditors are all other creditors. We we'll refer to them as John's personal (i.e., non-business) creditors. These are creditors outside of John's business. For example, if Mary decides she wants to divorce John, she becomes a personal creditor. Like most people John doesn't think about personal creditors because he can't imagine a situation where he would have problems with one.

The tradeoff between protection and flexibility.

Asset protection planning involves two competing ideas:

1. Protecting assets from creditors
2. Flexibility (having access to the assets at all times)

For example, John could give all of his assets to a relative, say his brother. That would be great protection from future creditors, because John would no longer own the assets. However, it would be awful in terms of flexibility, because John would lose all control over his assets. John should have a balance between protection and flexibility.

Asset protection is not hiding assets.

Contrary to popular belief, asset protection is not about hiding assets. Just the opposite is true: John should plan on showing everything he's done (where the assets are), if a creditor wants to see it. John can't legally protect his assets from current creditors. That's because every state has laws against *fraudulent conveyance*, which means it's against the law to transfer your assets in order to prevent a current creditor from getting his hands on them. Consequently, if you have current creditors, you carve out the amount you owe to them, and do your asset protection planning with your other assets.

The type of assets determines the asset protection method.

Mary and John's attorney explains to them that there are a number of tools used to protect assets from the claims of future creditors. The most common tools are as follows:

- Irrevocable trust
- Limited partnership
- Limited liability company
- Liability and property insurance
- Gifts

The attorney goes on to tell them that each asset is looked at separately to determine what particular asset protection tool should be used. Mary and John decide that at this time they just don't want to be personally liable for claims against John's business.

John's attorney chooses to protect John and Mary by setting up a limited liability company (LLC) to conduct John's construction business. Instead of John doing business as a sole proprietorship, he will now run his business out of an LLC. This creates several advantages:

- It gives good asset protection by protecting John's personal assets from the claims of his business creditors.

- It offers a lot of flexibility (i.e., John has access to the assets).

- It allows John to separate ownership of his business from control over it. (This is a key component that can be used to create a more sophisticated asset protection plan in the future.)

What is an LLC?

Beginning in the mid 1980's, states began allowing for the creation of a new type of business organization called a *limited liability company* (LLC). Limited liability companies joined other, more familiar forms of doing business such as sole proprietorships, partnerships, and corporations.

There are strong similarities between an LLC and a corporation. An LLC, like a corporation, is a creature of state law. For example, to form an LLC in Georgia, a document called *Articles of Organization* is required to be filed with the Georgia Secretary of State, along with a $100 fee. This process is analogous to the steps required for forming a Georgia corporation. Just like a corporation has a president, a limited liability company's counterpart is the manager. LLC's have *membership interest certificates* instead of stock certificates. Rather than stockholders, LLC's have members.

The key document that holds a limited liability company together is the *operating agreement*. The operating agreement is a contract between the manager and the members. The operating agreement should be written to meet the main goals of the members. For example, John is interested in asset protection, and he wants to always be in control of his business. Thus the operating agreement for John's LLC should name him as the manager and state that the manager controls the day to day operations of the business, including the distribution of profits. The operating agreement should also state that all the members must approve:

- The appointment of a new manager (i.e., president)
- The admittance of new members

- The sale of the LLC's major assets
- The liquidation of the LLC

Taxation of an LLC.

An LLC, unless it elects on IRS Form 8832 to be taxed as a corporation, does not pay income tax. An LLC with two or more members is taxed like a partnership. Some states, such as Georgia allow LLCs with only one member. A single member LLC is taxed like a sole proprietorship. All the income to the LLC flows through to its members who report that income on their individual tax returns. With an LLC, there is only one income tax, and that tax is paid by the LLC's members.

Creditor Protection.

*Protecting John's personal assets
from his business creditors.*

American businessmen have been using corporations to conduct business as far back as the early 1800s in order to protect their personal assets from their corporations' creditors. Corporate shareholders are not liable for a corporation's debts and other liabilities. An LLC is simply an updated version of a corporation.

The operating agreement of John's LLC appoints John as the manager. As manager, John still runs his business in the same way he did when he was a sole proprietor. The difference is that John is no longer personally liable for claims against his business. Once John's LLC begins doing business Mary and John will have met all of their estate planning goals.

Why use an LLC instead of a corporation?

Both LLC's and corporations protect personal assets from business creditors: The members of an LLC cannot lose their personal assets including their membership interest certificates to the creditors of their LLC. Likewise, the shareholders of a corporation cannot lose their personal assets including their stock certificates to the creditors of their corporation.

LLC's, however, have a unique feature: state law provides that LLC members cannot lose their membership interest certificates to their own personal creditors. Shareholders do not have this favorable protection. Shareholders can lose their corporate stock certificates to their own personal creditors as a result of losing a lawsuit for money damages.

LLC's, by themselves, are not the final word in asset protection, because under state law a personal creditor can file a lawsuit and obtain an economic interest in John's membership interest certificates. An economic interest allows a personal creditor to garnish the LLC's distributions to John, in much the same way that a creditor can garnish wages. Without additional planning, an LLC is only a roadblock to a creditor.

Multiple LLC's add additional asset protection for John's business.

As John's business grows to the point where he is simultaneously working on several large projects, his attorney may want to form a separate LLC for each of these projects. Thus, if one project fails or has creditor claims, the other projects won't be affected.

Protecting personal assets from personal creditors.

John was not interested in protecting his personal assets from his personal creditors. However, a simple way to protect your cash and stocks, is to transfer these assets to a single member LLC if your state allows this type of LLC. Your personal creditors cannot reach inside the LLC to obtain assets, but they can garnish LLC distributions paid to you. Although the LLC by itself is only a roadblock to a creditor, it is much better than doing nothing.

Is there a way to obtain more protection from personal creditors? There is by making a gift of membership interest certificates. However, to stay in control you'll need to use an LLC that has at least two members, rather than a single member LLC.

The big secret in asset protection planning is to separate ownership from control. LLC's and limited partnerships are the two entities used for this purpose. John controls the LLC as the manager, and initially he owns 100% of the membership interest certificates. John can then give away as much as 99% of the membership interest certificates, and still control the operation of the LLC. (As a 1% member John will continue to control the LLC because the Operating Agreement will say that all members must approve the appointment of a new manager.)

John's gift of 99% of his membership interests will create excellent asset protection: John's creditors will be unable to obtain an economic interest in the membership interest certificates he gives away because he will no longer own them. Also, under state law a personal creditor cannot reach into an LLC to collect a debt.

John has a number of choices to whom to give his membership interest certificates: an irrevocable trust for Mary, an irrevocable trust for his children, or an irrevocable trust for himself. If he wants to create a trust for himself he would have to do that in Alaska, Delaware, Utah, Nevada, Rhode Island, or an offshore tax haven.

For example, if John has a good marriage it would be easy for him to create a *simple trust* for the benefit of Mary. (A simple trust is an irrevocable trust that requires all *trust income* to be paid annually to its beneficiaries.) A good choice for trustee would be John's attorney or CPA. John can then give 99% of the membership interests to the trust, and keep 1% for himself. As manager John will continue to run the LLC, and decide when income is distributed to him and Mary. The downside to John is that under the federal tax law he cannot be paid a salary and will receive only 1% of the income distributions. Mary, however, as beneficiary of the simple trust, will receive 99% of the income distributions. As a practical matter if John wants to pay LLC income to Mary he doesn't have to run it through the simple trust. He can just pay her directly. When a simple trust is the owner of LLC membership interest certificates, this is how the majority of CPA's handle cash distributions of LLC income.

A work in progress.

Mary and John's estate plan is dynamic: it can adapt quickly to their changing goals, priorities and financial condition. Additional strategies will be added, as the need arises. For example, suppose John wants to make sure his business isn't thrown into chaos, if he suddenly dies. John's attorney can lay the framework for a solution by setting up a successor management team that would have legal authority to run John's business immediately upon his disability or death. John's construction foreman and his CPA could be the successor management team, and their authority to run the business could be added to the limited liability company documents. If John desires, he can name Mary as a member of the successor management team and even give her authority to fire the other managers. The point is that Mary and John's plan never has to become obsolete.

TEN

How to Care for Your Pets If You Become Incapacitated or Die

What can you do to protect your pets if one day you are unable to care for them? If you don't want to leave the care of your pets to chance, you will need a formal arrangement with a caregiver. This type of planning is very similar to what you'd do for the care of a minor child.

If you have a purebred dog or cat that is registered with a national association such as the American Kennel Club or the Cat Fancier's Association, you may have a simple solution: List two or more owners on the registration. In the event you become unable to care for your pet, a co-owner can become the caregiver. This is an excellent solution if your co-owner is eager and able to care for your pet.

Another good choice for a formal arrangement is to set up a trust for your pets. Pet trusts are a new idea and are written into law in only a handful of states. In these states, trusts for pets have the same validity as trusts for humans. In the other states, trusts created for pets are "honored," even though they are not technically enforceable under state law. If you choose to create a trust for you pets, put only enough money into the trust for the basic care and maintenance of your pets, because leaving excessive amounts may encourage relatives to contest the trust.

A trust for your pets should be created while you are living, and money should be immediately transferred to the trust. The trust can either be a separate document or a separate section of your revocable living trust. Just as if caring for a child, choose a trustee who is good at handling money, and select a caregiver who will love and care for your pets. The trustee and caregiver may be one and the same. In the trust you can list the name, address and phone number of your pets' veterinarian; provide information about dietary requirements; and give instructions on what should be done if the caregiver no longer desires to care for your pets. Provide your caregiver/trustee with a copy of your pet trust and keys to your home.

What if your caregiver can no longer continue caring for your pets? Although it would be best for your caregiver to place your pets with a loving family, that may not always be an option. In that event, you can include in your pets' trust a list of no kill animal shelters in your area. These no kill shelters, however, don't accept all pets. However, a no-kill shelter might accept your pet if it brought its own trust fund! (See www.saveourstrays.com for a nationwide list of these shelters.) You can also pre-arrange for your caregiver to send one or more of your pets to a pet retirement home such as the Bide-A-Wee Golden Years Retirement Home in New York (www.bideawee.org). Pet retirement homes require advance payments in the thousands of dollars and often accept only older pets.

A Will is not a good place to formalize your plans for the care of your pets. A Will doesn't come into effect if you are incapacitated; and if you die, it may be months before an executor is appointed. Your pets need immediate attention. They can't wait until the completion of the probate process before receiving basic care and funds.

The Humane Society of the United States has prepared an informative pamphlet, titled *Planning for Your Pet's Future Without You*, which is available at www.hsus.org. The pamphlet provides a thoughtful discussion on how to plan for your pets' care if something unexpected happens to you.

ELEVEN

Is There a Good Way to Plan for Long-Term Care?

MEDICARE

Except for a 100 day stay in a skilled nursing facility, Medicare will not pay for custodial care or room and board in an assisted living facility or nursing home.

The Original Medicare Plan

Medicare is the federal government health insurance program for persons 65 years and older, and for some others who are disabled. It has two parts: Part A and Part B.

Medicare Part A is free if you qualify for social security or railroad retirement benefits, and helps pay for inpatient care in a hospital, treatment in a skilled nursing facility, hospice care and some home health care.

Medicare Part B is medical insurance coverage that pays for medical expenses such as doctors' services (not routine physical exams),

X-rays, wheelchairs, physical therapy, speech therapy and some home health care. The insurance premium for Part B is $66.60 per month in 2004, and will rise based on how much the overall Medicare program's spending increases. The Part B premium is usually taken out of your monthly social security check.

You have to pay a portion of most Medicare-approved services. For each hospital stay up to 60 days you are charged $876 (in 2004). You are also charged 20% of most Medicare-approved services that are provided under Part B, after paying a $100 yearly deductible. To help pay these expenses and obtain more benefits you can purchase a Medigap health insurance policy. In most states there are 10 standardized Medigap policies sold by private insurance companies that provide different levels of benefits. The Medigap policy with the least benefits costs approximately $800 per year, and the most expensive policy costs about $4500 per year.

The Medicare-Plus-Choice Plan

Instead of getting your medical insurance coverage under the Original Medicare Plan, you can join a Medicare-Plus-Choice Plan. You must have Medicare Part A and Part B to join a Medicare-Plus-Choice Plan. Under some plans your monthly Part B premium is reduced. Depending on the area of the country you live in your choices may include:

- Medicare Managed Care Plans (HMO type plans)
- Medicare Private Fee-for-Service Plans (You can go to any doctor who accepts Medicare patients.)

Congress created the Medicare-Plus-Choice program to allow private insurance companies to provide more choices and extra benefits, such as prescription drugs, to Medicare patients. Congress has given billions of dollars to companies in the program. Unfortunately, premiums charged to patients in the Medicare-Plus Choice program continue to rise and benefits continue to shrink.

**Medicare does not pay for
custodial care in an assisted
living facility or nursing home.**

Neither the Original Medicare Plan nor the Medicare-Plus-Choice program pays for custodial care. Custodial care assists a person with the six activities of daily living:

- Getting out of bed
- Walking to the bathroom
- Using the toilet
- Bathing
- Dressing
- Eating

Medicare, however, can help pay for 100 days in a nursing home or other skilled nursing facility. The Medicare Part A nursing facility rules allow for full payment of the first twenty days and partial payment for the next eighty days at a skilled nursing facility during a continuous period of treatment. Skilled nursing facilities can be located at the extended care wing of a hospital or at a continuing-care retirement community, but are usually located in nursing homes. It isn't easy to meet the skilled nursing facility eligibility requirements because the rules require the following four conditions to be met:

- You have to first be in a hospital for 3 consecutive days, not including the day of discharge.
- Your doctor has to order daily care in a skilled nursing facility.
- You have to be admitted to a skilled nursing facility within 30 days of being discharged from the hospital.
- Your condition has to be "improving." Once your condition has stabilized, Medicare will stop paying for skilled nursing facility care, no matter how serious your condition is at that time.

Medicare-Plus-Choice Plans often have less stringent rules and may not require a 3 consecutive day hospital stay in order to be admitted to a skilled nursing facility. For more information about Medicare health plans look on the web at www.medicare.gov.

A Medicare-certified home care agency will provide home health care.

Some home health care is available under both Medicare Part A and Part B and the Medicare-Plus Choice Plans. This care is provided at home, an adult day care center, or an assisted living facility. Home health care helps pay for services such as physical therapy, part-time skilled nursing care, and speech therapy. Home health care also helps pay for medical equipment, including wheelchairs, oxygen, and walkers.

At first glance the rules to obtain home health care appear difficult to meet: You must be recovering from an injury or illness and the care must be ordered by your doctor, be performed by a Medicare-certified home care agency, and be medically necessary in Medicare's opinion. In practice the certified home care agencies perform these services on a regular basis, and file the necessary claim forms to get paid.

A New Medicare Benefit — Prescription Drugs

New legislation that became law in December 2003 creates a Medicare prescription drug plan to begin in 2006. The initial enrollment period for Medicare beneficiaries to sign up for the drug plan begins on November 15, 2005 and will likely end seven months later. The Medicare website, www.medicare.gov, will contain the details of the enrollment process.

The drug benefit is convoluted. The initial premium is expected to be $35 per month. After a $250 deductible is met, insurance will pay 75% of the next $2000 of drug costs. The next $2850 aren't covered. After that, insurance will pay 95% of each prescription.

The expected $35 monthly premium will likely rise in the future because the premium is determined by a formula that is tied to increases in drug costs. Congress did nothing in the legislation to hold down drug costs.

The big winners are Medicare beneficiaries with high drug needs or low incomes. Under the new plan, the Medicare beneficiary who spends $3000 a year on prescription drugs will save about 44%, after taking into account the $420 yearly premium. The person who spends ten to fifteen thousand a year, will save substantially more.

Low-income Medicare beneficiaries with annual incomes below about $13,000 ($17,000 for a couple) will only have to pay $1 to $5 per prescription. They won't be asked to pay a premium or a deductible. Income, however, is broadly defined and includes social security benefits. Seniors who have more than $6000 in assets ($9000 for a couple) excluding a house and car, will not qualify for this subsidy.

Congress envisions that some seniors will stay in original Medicare and enroll in a Prescription Drug Plan. The prescription drug plans are private insurance plans that will contract with Medicare to provide drug coverage. Other seniors may leave original Medicare and join a private health insurance plan, known as the Medicare Advantage Plan, that will offer drug coverage and other medical benefits. The Medicare Advantage Plan will be a local health maintenance organization (HMO) or a regional preferred provider organization (PPO). In areas that don't have at least one stand-alone drug plan and one Medicare Advantage HMO or PPO, seniors will be able to buy drug coverage directly from Medicare. The private plans that have contracts with Medicare will receive monthly payments from Medicare.

To keep costs down, the private plans will most likely limit the drugs that will be covered and require the use of older drugs and generics instead of costlier new drugs. A senior who lives in an area that has more than one plan should shop for the plan that covers the particular drugs he needs.

Although it's optional to enroll in a Prescription Drug Plan or Medicare Advantage Plan, a Medicare beneficiary will be penalized with higher premiums if he waits to sign up. (There won't be a penalty for signing up late if the Medicare beneficiary already has drug coverage from another source, such as from a former employer.)

After January 1, 2006 a person won't be able to buy a Medigap health insurance policy that pays for prescription drugs. However, a senior who already owns a Medigap policy that pays for drugs will be allowed to renew his Medigap policy. If he later enrolls in a Prescription Drug Plan or Medicare Advantage Plan, he will lose the drug portion of his Medigap policy.

MEDICAID

Medicaid will pay for long-term care in a nursing home, but only if you're poor.

Often confused with Medicare, Medicaid is the jointly-funded federal and state medical assistance program for the financially needy. State and local governments administer Medicaid, within broad federal guidelines. Eligibility rules, regulations and benefits vary greatly from state to state.

What does Medicaid cover?

Provided you meet the eligibility requirements, Medicaid will pay for the same services as Medicare and more. For example, Medicaid will pay for custodial care in a nursing home, daily visits to an adult day care center (including transportation), and home health care if you want to remain in your own home rather than be institutionalized in a nursing home. Medicaid will not pay for room and board in an assisted living facility, but in some states, it will pay for medical services provided there.

Who is eligible for Medicaid?

Each state has different eligibility rules to determine which financially needy people qualify for medical assistance. In general to qualify for Medicaid, the cost of your medical care must exceed what you can afford, and you must spend most of your savings. Each month you will have to use all but a few hundred dollars of your income, including your retirement income and social security, to pay for your nursing home and medical bills. Medicaid will then pay the unpaid balance. Federal law requires states to institute programs to recover Medicaid costs from the estates of deceased recipients. Every state has an estate recovery program.

You can keep exempt assets.

The Medicaid rules allow an applicant to keep certain exempt assets and still qualify for Medicaid. Although the rules are different in each state, an unmarried person can generally keep the following assets:

- A home of any value
- A prepaid funeral contract up to $5,000
- A car, household goods, and furniture
- Some types of life insurance
- Some types of income producing property, such as rental real estate
- Pensions, annuities and IRAs that are already paying out income
- Additional assets of $2,000

If the Medicaid nursing home applicant is married, the spouse remaining at home can keep assets of up to $90,660 in 2003 (adjusted annually for inflation based on the Consumer Price Index), plus assets that generally include:

- A home of any value
- A prepaid funeral contract up to $5,000
- A car, household goods, and furniture

- Some types of life insurance
- Some types of income producing property, such as rental real estate

Furthermore, in some states the income of the stay-at-home spouse has no effect on the Medicaid eligibility of the nursing home spouse. The spouse who resides in the nursing home can generally keep pensions, annuities, and IRAs that are already paying out income, a prepaid funeral contract up to $5,000, and additional assets of $2,000.

Transfers of assets.

Medicaid allows an applicant to make a few specific asset transfers without any penalty, including transfers to a spouse or a disabled child. Other transfers by the Medicaid applicant must occur more than 36 months (60 months if assets are transferred to most types of trusts) prior to applying for Medicaid. Violation of the 36/60-month asset-transfer rules causes time penalties to be imposed that can significantly delay Medicaid eligibility.

What is Medicaid planning?

Medicaid planning is a relatively new legal specialty that helps people preserve assets for their spouse and children, and still qualify for Medicaid long-term care benefits. Medicaid planning is mostly nursing home planning. The American public has become reliant on Medicaid to pay nursing home costs. The cost of nursing home care is skyrocketing, and many Americans don't want to spend their last dime paying these expenses.

Most people don't know about the rules and regulations that allow them to keep their house and other types of assets, and still have Medicaid pay for their nursing home care. The best nursing homes, even though they may be Medicaid providers, don't want Medicaid patients, and discriminate against them at the time of admission. Few states have laws preventing this. So don't think that all you have to do for

Medicaid planning is to give your children all your assets, wait 36 months, and then check in to a desirable nursing home. To get into a desirable nursing home you will have to be admitted as a private patient, after first showing that you have substantial assets or long-term care insurance. Then, if you want to do Medicaid planning, you will have to enlist the services of a Medicaid attorney to protect your assets for your family and at the same time make you eligible for Medicaid. Under federal law, a nursing home can't kick out a Medicaid patient who has already been admitted.

Medicaid attorneys.

There are only a handful of competent lawyers in each state who devote their practice to Medicaid planning, and it is not easy to find them. Their help is sought, either by someone who wants to plan for future nursing home care as part of their estate planning, or more frequently by a family in the midst of a crisis involving a spouse or parent already in or about to enter a nursing home. Just because a lawyer holds himself out as an elder-law attorney, does not mean that he is proficient in Medicaid planning. Your attorney needs to know the federal and state Medicaid rules and regulations backwards and forwards. Many applications for Medicaid are denied. Consequently, Medicaid lawyers must file appeals and argue their clients' cases before state administrative law judges. If you are not indigent, expect to pay a lot for the services of a top Medicaid lawyer.

CHOOSING A LONG-TERM CARE INSURANCE POLICY

Long-term care policies provide security if you become severely disabled or chronically ill.

Long-term care insurance mostly pays for custodial care, including a place to live and help with the six activities of daily living.

Because of the high cost of caring for people who have a stroke, Alzheimer's, or a prolonged illness, it makes sense to purchase a long-term care insurance policy if you can afford it. The policies, however, are difficult to understand, and may not pay the benefits you expect. You don't just call up your insurance agent and tell him that you decided to move into an assisted living facility and expect your policy to pay the bill. Insurance companies won't pay any benefits unless you can prove that you are chronically ill or severely disabled. Nevertheless, you may be able to get the policy you want if you know what to look for.

There's nothing simple about choosing a long-term care policy. You can't rely on the slick sales brochures, or on the salesman's promises. And unless you are extremely well informed about long-term care insurance, you won't know what questions to ask your agent. It's not only the options you choose when you fill out the insurance application that effect your long-term care coverage, it's also the fine print in the policy that determines if your long-term care bills get paid. You can see the fine print before you purchase the insurance by asking your agent for a copy of the policy. The following is a crash course in what to consider when you're purchasing a policy.

Buy from a large company.

You need to purchase your long-term care insurance from a large, financially stable insurance company that has assets in the billions. You'll need the company to out last you, if you expect to collect benefits.

What is the true price of your policy?

It is important to compare the price of long-term care policies, because polices with similar features have large variations in prices. A knowledgeable, trustworthy insurance agent can help you.

If you want to compare prices on your own, the Weiss ratings website, www.weissratings.com, provides useful information and a free questionnaire to help you determine which features to choose. For a fee, the Weiss ratings site will prepare a customized report of companies in your area showing each policy's features, including comparisons of policy premiums and company financial ratings. But that is not the end of the story.

With long-term care insurance you are making a mistake if you are trying to buy the cheapest policy from a company that you never heard of. A cheap policy from an unknown company will probably guarantee that your premiums will increase and that the company won't be in the long-term care business when you need your benefits.

Some companies have a history of frequently raising premiums. Others that are new to the market haven't had enough experience to know how to price their products. The sales pitch, that you can't be singled out for rate hikes and the only rate increases will be those applied to members of the same class, is meaningless. The term "class" is nebulous and can be interpreted any way the insurance company wishes to justify rate increases at will. The policy that has lower premiums in the beginning, may actually wind up costing you more, eventually pricing you out of the market and causing your policy to be canceled.

As you would expect your health is an important factor in determining the premium you will be quoted. When you are purchasing a policy your agent may quote the lower preferred rate. Don't be surprised if the insurance company, after reviewing your application, wants you to pay a higher premium because of questions about your health.

The cost of long-term care.

People commonly underestimate the cost of long-term care so they don't buy enough coverage. If you haven't checked into the cost of nursing homes, assisted living, home health-care services and adult day care in your area, you may be in for a surprise.

According to the 2002 MetLife Market Survey, the average yearly cost for a private room in a nursing home is $61,320. The average hourly rate for home health care is $37 for a Licensed Practical Nurse and $18 for a home health aid. Based on our own experience with our family, a couple who wants to live in an assisted living facility should plan on paying $5,000 to $6,000 per month for room, board, and the appropriate level of care.

What "triggers" (conditions you will be required to prove in order to obtain benefits) are included in your policy?

Congress decided in 1996 that certain long-term care insurance policies should be treated for income tax purposes like health insurance policies: a portion of the premiums are deductible and the benefits are tax exempt. Policies that conform to Congress's definition of a long-term care policy are eligible for these tax advantages and are referred to as tax-qualified policies by insurance companies. For people who are not terminally ill, there is a maximum amount of benefits that can be received tax-free. In 2003 the maximum amount was $220 per day.

Most long-term care policies that are sold today are tax-qualified policies that pay benefits only if a licensed health care practitioner certifies in writing that you require either:

- "substantial assistance" to perform two of the activities of daily living for at least 90 days due to a loss of functional capacity, or
- "substantial supervision" to protect yourself from threats to health and safety due to severe cognitive (i.e., mental) impairment

Each of the above requirements is called a trigger. These two triggers are found in all tax-qualified policies. If you meet one of the triggers you will qualify for benefits. Practically speaking, unless your doctor and the insurance company's doctor agree that you will require at least 90 days of substantial assistance with two of the activities of daily living, you won't be eligible to receive your long-term care benefits. It becomes their subjective decision.

Non tax-qualified policies can contain triggers that make it easier to obtain benefits. These policies, however, are hard to find. That's understandable because it is unclear whether the proceeds from non tax-qualified policies are exempt from federal income tax.

Where will you end up receiving care?

You need to decide where you will want to receive your care: nursing home, assisted living, continuing-care retirement community, at home or a combination of all four. Your policy should explicitly permit all types of facilities, but the problem is that there is no standard definition for these care settings. The terms vary from policy to policy, and even among state regulators. Look carefully at how your policy defines "assisted living facility" and "adult day care center" and make sure these accurately describe the facilities in your area. If you move out of state after purchasing your policy, it may not cover the type of facility you may want in your new state.

You also need the right to select from a range of services appropriate to each setting. For example if you prefer home care, your policy should offer such services as health care, personal care, nutrition, homemaking and more, from a licensed home health care professional, family member or friend. If your policy requires you to use only certified care providers, then you won't be able to pay your family members who are helping to take care of you. Your policy should not force you prematurely into a nursing home if you prefer not to be there.

Who will manage your care?

Can you decide for yourself what your care plan will be, or are you required to use a care manager who can act as a gatekeeper determining what services you will receive? There is a big debate in the insurance industry as to whether a care manager is acting in your best interest, or in the interest of the insurance company. Do you anticipate needing help finding services at a reasonable price, or do you think you or a family member can handle this on your own? Do you want to receive a fixed daily dollar amount (e.g., $120 per day) to be spent as you see fit (indemnity-type policy)? Or would you rather have a care manager pay only for the actual services he approves up to a daily maximum per day, for example $120 per day, (reimbursement type policy)? You'll have to make a decision as to what type of policy to buy — indemnity, reimbursement, or a hybrid of the two — but there are no clear-cut best choices. The majority of the policies sold are the reimbursement type.

Selecting a waiting period.

You will have to select a waiting period (the initial time when you have to pay your own long-term care expenses). The way your policy calculates your waiting period has a significant impact on the interval between the onset of your disability and the time you can begin collecting benefits. You'll be out of pocket for your long-term care expenses during that period. How long will you have to satisfy your waiting period and how is it calculated? During the waiting period, how many days per week will you have to receive care, for example two out of seven, for it to be counted the same as seven days of disability? Suppose you choose a 90-day waiting period, will you have 90, 180, or 360 days to accumulate your required 90 days of disability before having to start a new waiting period? And how many waiting periods do you have to satisfy during your lifetime, if you get better and there is a break in the time you are classified as disabled? Some policies say you have to satisfy only one waiting period in your lifetime, while others require more.

Inflation Protection.

Inflation protection is designed to increase the dollar amount of your daily benefit in an attempt to keep pace with the increase in long-term care costs over time. In most policies you can add an inflation rider to your policy that annually increases your daily benefit by 5 percent, using either a simple interest or compounded interest calculation.

The simple interest calculation means that each year your original daily benefit will increase by five percent. If your original daily benefit is $100, each year your daily benefit will increase by $5. In other words, in twenty years your daily benefit will have doubled.

Under the compounded interest calculation, your inflation increase is five percent of the previous year's daily benefit. Assuming an original daily benefit of $100, under the compounded interest calculation you initially multiply five percent times $100 to determine that your daily benefit will increase by $5. However, for the next year's calculation you multiply five percent times $105, resulting in an increase of $5.25. Using the compounded method your daily benefit will double in fifteen years.

Reducing the amount of annual premiums.

If you can afford to pay premiums for long-term care insurance without affecting your lifestyle, then start buying lifetime coverage at age fifty. At that age you can probably qualify for preferred rates, and the annual premiums will be a lot less expensive than if you wait until age sixty or sixty-five to purchase a policy.

Don't buy long-term care insurance thinking that the insurance will pay for all of your custodial care. Also, factor in your expected social security benefits, retirement income, and maybe other assets you will want to use to pay for your long-term care, and buy insurance to provide for the difference.

A common way to reduce premiums is to buy a policy that pays benefits for four, six or ten years rather than for life. Companies also sell policies that last only two years, although that is probably too short a time period to protect you.

If you expect that it will be 15 or 20 years before needing to use your policy, inflation protection is important to guarantee that your policy will be sufficient to pay your bills. An inflation rider, however, usually doubles the amount of the yearly premium. If you are first purchasing a policy at age 70, an inflation rider may price the policy out of your budget. In such a case don't buy the inflation protection. Instead try to anticipate future inflation by purchasing a policy with a higher daily benefit than you normally would have purchased.

Filing claims and collecting benefits.

How easy is it to file your claims and collect your benefits? Are there 800 numbers for service representatives available 24 hours a day, and how long will it take the company to process your claims? Some experts think that this is the most important consideration in buying a long-term care policy. Perhaps the claims history of the company with other types of insurance would be a valuable indicator in trying to predict how your claims will be handled. If you can obtain accurate information from your agent about the percentage of long-term care claims that the company has actually paid, that would be helpful, too.

Conclusion.

Purchasing long-term care insurance can be as bewildering as purchasing a car, and probably more so. You've got to invest time at the front end investigating policy features and prices if you want the desired result: an affordable policy that pays benefits to you when you're expecting them.

TWELVE

The Great Hunt for
An Estate Planning Attorney

How will you know that you've found the right estate planning attorney? You won't. Only upon your death and in the years that follow will it become apparent that you chose, or failed to choose, the right attorney to help you in your estate planning. But it's not hopeless. You can improve the odds that your estate plan will turn out the way you want by doing some legwork on the front end.

Lawyers don't hang out shingles that tell you their estate planning method and biases. If you have a chronic backache, you know the kind of treatment you can expect if you go to a chiropractor, an acupuncturist, an orthopedist, or a physical therapist. But it takes considerable effort on your part to uncover an estate planning attorney's personal biases in the documents he chooses for estate plans. If for example, you have decided that you want to avoid probate, you'll want to choose an attorney who is disposed and experienced to do just that.

Writing an estate plan and the associated documents is closer to an art than a science. There is often more than one way to accomplish the same set of goals. Just as you can take a Volkswagen chassis and, with enough modifications, turn it into a Porsche, you can take the traditional Will, and add enough bells and whistles so that it will offer many of the same kinds of benefits often found in a properly designed revocable living trust. The difficulty with this approach is in finding an attorney knowledgeable enough to carry it off, at an affordable cost.

Price is not a good indicator of quality.

If you go shopping for an attorney based on price alone, you'll more than likely be comparing apples to oranges. It's not like you're searching around for the best deal on a particular model car with a given set of options. It's more like you're asking for a quote on a new roof for your home. One roofer will first replace any damaged wood, fill nail holes, put down tarpaper and select a high-quality shingle. Another roofer will just rip off the old shingles and replace them with low quality shingles. Your home will have a new roof and may look cosmetically beautiful, at least for the time being, using either roofer. And the prices of the two roofers may not be all that different, but the end result definitely is. The difference is in the quality of their work.

If you're concerned about quality, don't go shopping around for the lowest-priced Will or revocable living trust. If you've been quoted less than $1,000 for a revocable living trust, it's probably not worth the paper it's written on. However, just because an attorney charges more doesn't mean he's going to give you a better product.

Where to begin your search for the right estate planning attorney.

If you are fortunate enough to live in a state where the state bar awards certification to attorneys in estate planning, then some of the guesswork is taken out of the process. You can phone the state bar association for a list of attorneys who have met the minimum competency standards to call themselves estate planners. Your list of possible candidates is narrowed, but you are far from finished.

If, in your state, as in the majority of states, there are no certification standards for estate planning attorneys, then you need some other means to arrive at an initial pool of possible candidates. In such cases anyone can call himself an estate planner, without any of the necessary training or experience. A *Yellow Pages* listing under a related category such as Wills, trusts and probate, provides no assurances of an attorney's qualifications.

Referral sources — not always a step in the right direction.

Attorneys you already know.

You've probably already made a relationship with one or more attorneys, either socially or on a professional basis. You might know some from your neighborhood, your church or previous dealings such as real estate closings and business relationships. No matter how much you may like the attorney, unless he devotes his entire practice to estate planning, then that attorney is not right for you. Just as you wouldn't let your internist perform brain surgery on you, you need to select a specialist in estate planning to design and execute your estate plan.

Estate planning is such a complex field that you cannot get a high level of expertise from someone who dabbles in it only part time. A law school graduate only has the rudimentary knowledge to begin learning about estate planning. Competency in estate planning is developed outside of law school by learning from other lawyers, attending seminars, reading books and articles, and gaining practical experience from years of designing estate plans and drafting estate planning documents. The field is dynamic because of continual changes in the Internal Revenue Code, Internal Revenue Service regulations, proposed regulations, and IRS letter rulings. An attorney must stay abreast with an ever-changing field. Someone who doesn't devote his practice entirely to estate planning will not have the time to make this level of educational commitment.

Referrals from friends.

The same cautionary remarks that apply to attorneys you already know apply to referrals from friends as well. However, if your friend has found an attorney whose entire practice is devoted to estate planning, and your friend was satisfied with the product that attorney produced, the recommendation has merit.

Referrals from financial planners, insurance agents, and CPA's.

Financial planners and insurance agents aren't disinterested parties. They usually have products to sell and are not likely to refer you to attorneys who aren't supporters of their wares. Although your CPA is your trusted advisor, he may not know any more about estate planning than you do. This doesn't mean that these advisors can't put you in touch with the right attorney; it's just not something you can take for granted.

Estate planning services as part of a bundled financial or insurance package.

When estate planning documents are "free" or sold as part of a "package" which includes life insurance, financial products, etc. you can assume that the estate planning documents are only incidental to the sale of the other products. Volume is paramount over quality in these trust mill operations. You shouldn't expect a customized plan that is tailored to your particular needs, nor should you expect to be able to determine the expertise of the attorney who will be drafting your documents. If your quality expectations and the fee you're willing to pay are both in the low range, then you may be satisfied with the result. However, it is more likely that you are about to make a costly mistake.

Networks, estate planning councils and other professional organizations.

Networks, estate planning councils and other professional organizations have members who have an avowed interest in estate planning. Their membership privileges vary, but can include offering seminars, subscriptions to special estate planning journals, and specialized software packages that assist in drafting documents to meet each client's individual needs. Some examples of these organizations are:

- American College of Trust and Estate Counsel (www.actec.org)
- National Association of Estate Planners and Councils (NAEPC) (www.naepc.org)
- The National Network of Estate Planning Attorneys, Inc. (www.netplanning.com)

Just about every major city in the U.S. has one or more local estate planning councils, and their addresses can be found on the NAEPC website.

References from an attorney's existing clients.

When an attorney handles a divorce case, a real estate closing, or drafts a business contract, etc., the client knows in a relatively short period if that attorney's services are to his liking. But the outcome of an estate plan will rarely be known until after the death or disability of one or more spouses. Other than learning if the attorney performed the work in a timely manner, was cordial, and was accessible to answer questions, there isn't a whole lot to be gained from interviewing an attorney's other clients. It is doubtful that existing clients would want to reveal such personal, but relevant, financial information as the size of their estate or details of their plan. Most clients lack the knowledge and expertise to objectively evaluate the quality of the documents they receive, and so their opinions are largely a matter of guesswork. But if it will make you feel better to speak to a few existing clients, by all means ask for some references.

Narrowing down the field — questions to ask.

This is a tough one because everybody has different goals. If you simply want to leave everything to your spouse and hope for the best, you don't need to search out an attorney who is an estate planning specialist. However, if your goals are more extensive and you want results that are guaranteed, then you'll need the help of an attorney with considerable estate planning expertise.

What percentage of your practice is devoted to estate planning?
For how many years has that percentage been going on?

The answers to these questions will give you a good idea about the attorney's estate planning experience. Experienced estate planning attorneys devote one hundred percent of their practice to estate planning. You don't want your family doctor to perform your heart bypass. Neither should you depend on an attorney who doesn't devote his practice to estate planning to draw up your plan and draft the necessary documents. The whole point of doing an estate plan is to increase the odds that you will accomplish your set of goals; so why accept less than the best?

How much of the estate planning portion of
your practice is devoted to Wills and probate?

You have already learned that for many estate planning attorneys, Wills, probate and the preparation of the federal estate tax return are the cash cows that feed their practice. Attorneys who have a Will/ probate practice like to write Wills. They have not been trained to prepare and fund quality revocable living trusts, and usually have no desire to learn. Wills guarantee probate, and the probate lawyer will steer you toward a Will because that is what he prepares. The main point is that the estate planning attorney you choose should educate you about estate planning; and you, rather than your attorney, should make the choice if you want to go the Will/probate route.

How much of the estate planning portion of
your practice is devoted to revocable living trusts?

If you get a positive response to this question, you are probably speaking with an attorney who is set up for living trust work and enjoys preparing these trusts. If you like the estate planning process described in this book, you should hire an attorney who specializes in revocable living trusts to help you with your planning. The National Network of Estate Planning Attorneys is an organization which trains its members in the living trust process. Its address is in Appendix D. If you are sure that a Will is best for you, there is no need to get in contact with one of these attorneys.

If you are considering a living trust, but are not sure you really need one, ask the living trust attorney the following question: *If my estate planning goals can be met with a Will, rather than a living trust, will you prepare a Will for a reasonable fee or refer me to someone who can?* If you get a yes, then you can meet with the attorney to decide if he or she is right for you.

Do you have a standard document for my situation?
(for example, a married couple with two children)

If the attorney answers yes, your antennae should go up. If you are looking for estate planning based on your specific goals for your family, you are most likely speaking to the wrong attorney. It is a rare occurrence when a man can go into a store, purchase an off the rack suit, and have it look like it was custom made for him. More than likely the suit will require alteration, to more approximate the made-to-measure variety. The same is true for estate planning documents. A boilerplate draft may be a good first approximation to your final document, but rarely will it be perfectly suited without further modification to meet your particular needs.

*If my estate plan includes a revocable living
trust, will you fund it for me?*

No question is more important than this one. Just as a Will is a
useless piece of paper if it doesn't control any of your assets, a trust
that doesn't control any assets is equally worthless. The process of
transferring your property to your trust is called funding. It can involve:

- Preparation of deeds to transfer real estate
- Changing the name on your money market and brokerage
  accounts
- Transfer of corporate stock certificates
- Assignment of limited partnership interests
- Changing beneficiaries of your life insurance policies
- Sometimes changing beneficiaries of your IRA accounts

For income and estate tax planning purposes it is important to
know which assets to transfer to your living trust, and which assets to
leave alone. It is equally important to correctly title your assets in the
name of your trust and to inform all interested parties, such as your
homeowner's insurance carrier and mortgage lender (if you are transferring a residence to a living trust). Funding is such an important step
that it is worth the price to have it done professionally, rather than risk
a costly error. Because it is time consuming, some estate planning attorneys will tell you to fund it yourself. Don't fall for this, because it is
a bad idea. Without proper training and experience it is unlikely you'll
be able to correctly fund your trust. The best way to get your assets
into your living trust is for the attorney who prepared it to promptly
fund your trust for you. Be prepared to pay additional fees for the
service. It is well worth the price to get the job done right!

If you choose to use a Will as your main estate planning document, the attorney chosen by your executor will change the title to
your assets after your death. Your Will determines who receives your
assets. This is where probate can become costly because you will not
be available to provide the attorney with documents that show the

assets you own. The probate attorney will have to find your assets without your help. Transferring title to assets is particularly time consuming when the owner is no longer alive to help with the process.

Do you charge by the hour or is there a
flat fee for the documents you prepare?

If you really want to let yourself in for a surprise, then agree to have your estate planning attorney bill by the hour. We hope by now you have an appreciation of the tremendous amount of time it takes to do a proper estate plan and execute the corresponding documents. If an estate planning attorney charges for all the time he spends on your plan you'll be startled when you receive the bill. It's far better to know what the attorney fees and any other costs will be, up front, so that you can choose how to proceed. You may wish to do the whole estate plan, do the plan in stages, or choose only to focus on your most important goals (to keep the fees to a minimum). You need an attorney who will present all the options and the cost of each so that you can make an informed decision.

Unless you have an extremely large estate you should be able to find an attorney willing to meet with you and design your plan for free. His charges then would be for the documents he prepares to implement the plan he designed for you.

Will you be contacting me to update my plan, on an annual basis?

Your relationship with your estate planning attorney is a lot like a marriage — till death do you part. You should enter into the relationship expecting it to last for the long term. You need your estate planning attorney to make sure that any new assets acquired over the past year are titled correctly. He needs to know if there have been any major changes in your family or in your financial situation that would necessitate modifications to your plan. And he will need to amend your trust(s) as legal requirements change.

Of course, as in marriage, there can be a parting of the ways, due to irreconcilable differences. But you should enter into a relationship with the idea that it is for the long haul. You should feel comfortable with your attorney, and confident in his legal expertise. This is some-one who is going to continue to play a part in your legal affairs, for many years to come.

Does the ideal estate planning attorney even exist?

The ideal estate planning attorney will identify your goals, and honestly tell you what you need. There are a lot of estate planning attorneys who will do this. The problem is that they are hard to find. Compounding the problem is that it's hard to tell the difference be-tween salesmanship and good, honest advice. But the closer you come to finding an estate planning attorney who approximates the ideal, the better your chances for a desirable outcome. A successful search is definitely worth the effort.

CONCLUSION

Most people believe that, to fully protect their loved ones, all they need is a Will and life insurance. They've bought into the big myth. This traditional approach to estate planning continues to reign in popu-larity only because few have stopped to examine its validity. Belief in other related myths has contributed to this tunnel vision style of think-ing when people are planning for their family's future well-being and prosperity. The common misconceptions about estate planning are:

- Your Will protects your family
- Naming a guardian is sufficient to take care of your minor children
- Your assets have to paid outright to your loved ones in ei-ther one lump sum, or at specified age intervals

- Probate is no big deal
- Estate taxes have been repealed
- There are no consequences for procrastinating in estate planning
- Your life insurance is guaranteed to protect your family
- In the event of an emergency, your hospital will have a copy of your living will and health care power of attorney
- Your estate is safe in the hands of your family members and attorney
- Family members or friends will take care of your pets if you become incapacitated or die
- Medicare and your other insurance will pay for your long-term care

Whereas the traditional approach assumes Wills and life insurance provide umbrella protection, in reality they leave nearly everything to chance. The fix for this problem is an alternative approach that targets your specific goals with tools and strategies that work. For example, if you want to guarantee that your assets will get to your spouse and children, protect your assets from future creditors, protect your children's inheritance from their failed marriages, and guarantee the avoidance of a court appointed guardian in the event you become mentally disabled, an expert estate planning attorney can do all that. But he can't do it using Wills and life insurance alone.

The alternative approach to estate planning follows a pattern that you're already familiar with. The pattern is a logical one, and it is similar to eating at a restaurant. You select a restaurant based on the chef's area of expertise or type of food served. If you're in the mood for sushi, you go to a Japanese restaurant that specializes in sushi, rather than to an Italian restaurant. When you arrive at the restaurant, and the waiter asks for your order, you don't tell him food. The chef would be clueless as to what to prepare. Nor does the chef decide the courses for you. Instead, you examine the choices and select from the menu. The waiter brings your order to the expert chef, who then prepares the meal based on what you want. The menu comes with prices so that you won't be surprised at the end of the meal. It's a sensible sequence of events that should be applied to estate planning.

The alternative approach to estate planning does just that. First you search for an expert estate planning attorney, rather than a generalist, and find one who is trained to prepare the types of documents that will do what you want. Your menu of options is the goals checklist. You become aware of your options and choose the types of protection you want for your family. Based on your choices, your expert estate planner designs your estate plan and drafts the necessary documents. To help you make your decisions about how you want to protect your family, your estate planning attorney informs you of the cost of accomplishing each of your goals. The result is an estate plan which meets your expectations rather than what your attorney decides for you. The documents replace wishful thinking with guaranteed results. It's a wonder that such a logical process is the exception rather than the norm.

We've proposed a new gold standard for estate planning. When implemented properly, this process will vastly improve the likelihood that you get what you have been expecting from estate planning (but never receiving from Wills) all along.

APPENDIX A

Will of John Hardy

On the following pages, you will find an example of a typical, simple Will that the vast majority of attorneys would consider perfectly good as long as a provision were added to include Mary and John's expected third child. However, the hidden problem that even most attorneys don't realize, is that this Will doesn't protect John's family, for the following reasons:

- *The Will does not control the disposition of most of his major assets, such as his house, stocks, 401(k) plan, and life insurance*
- *It provides no meaningful instructions for the care of his minor children*
- *It does not guarantee that his assets will get to his children*
- *It does not protect his children from losing their inheritance to their creditors or their failed marriages*

LAST WILL AND TESTAMENT
OF
JOHN HARDY

Introductory Clauses

I, JOHN HARDY, a resident of and domiciled in the County of Fulton and State of Georgia, do hereby make, publish and declare this to be my Last Will and Testament, hereby revoking all Wills and Codicils at any time heretofore made by me.

My spouse's name is MARY HARDY. All references to "my spouse" in this Will are to her.

I have two children: MICHAEL R. HARDY, born February 24, 1996; and KEVIN T. HARDY, born March 15, 1998.

ITEM I

Payment of Debts

I direct that all my legally enforceable debts, secured and unsecured, be paid as soon as practicable after my death.

ITEM II

General Bequest of Personal and Household Effects

I give and bequeath all my personal and household effects of every kind including but not limited to furniture, appliances, furnishings, pictures, silverware, china, glass, books, jewelry, wearing apparel, boats, automobiles, and other vehicles, and all policies of fire, burglary, property damage, and other insurance on or in connection with the use of this property, to my spouse, MARY HARDY, if she shall survive me. If my spouse shall not survive me, I give and bequeath all this property to my children surviving me in approximately equal shares. If any beneficiary hereunder is a minor, my Executor may distribute such minor's share to such minor or for such minor's use to any person with whom such minor is residing or who has care and control of such minor without further responsibility and the receipt of the person to whom it is distributed shall be a complete discharge by my Executor.

ITEM III

Specific Devise of Residential Property

I give and devise to my spouse, MARY HARDY, if she shall survive me, any interest which I own at the time of my death in the house and lot which I occupy as my residence at the time of my death. If this property at the time of my death is subject to any mortgage, then this devise shall be subject thereto and the devisee shall not be entitled to have the obligation secured by such mortgage paid out of my general estate. If my spouse shall not survive me, such property shall be added to and disposed of as part of my residuary estate.

ITEM IV

Distribution of My Residuary Estate

I give, devise and bequeath all the rest, residue and remainder of my property of every kind and description (including lapsed legacies and devises), wherever situate and whether acquired before or after the execution of this Will (hereinafter called my residuary estate) to my spouse if she shall survive me.

If my spouse shall not survive me, but issue of mine shall survive me, then I give, devise and bequeath all of my residuary estate to my Trustee to be held in trust, as follows:

Section 1. Division into Separate Shares

All property not previously distributed under the provisions of my Will shall be held in trust and divided as follows:

Beneficiary	Relationship	Share
Michael R. Hardy	Son	½
Kevin T. Hardy	Son	½

Section 2. Distribution of Trust Shares for My Children

The share of each child who survives me shall be distributed as follows:

a. Distribution of Trust Share for Michael R. Hardy

The trust share for MICHAEL R. HARDY shall be held in trust and administered and distributed as follows:

1. Distributions of Net Income and Principal

My Trustee, in its sole and absolute discretion, shall pay to, or apply for the benefit of, MICHAEL R. HARDY as much of the net income and principal from his trust share as my Trustee deems advisable for his education, health, maintenance, and support.

When MICHAEL R. HARDY reaches the age of 25, or if on the creation of his trust, he has already attained the age of 25, my Trustee shall distribute 1/2 of the trust accumulated net income and principal, as it is then constituted, to MICHAEL R. HARDY, free of the trust.

When MICHAEL R. HARDY reaches the age of 30,

or if on the creation of his trust, he has already attained the age of 30, my Trustee shall distribute the remaining balance of the trust accumulated net income and principal, as it is then constituted, to MICHAEL R. HARDY, free of the trust.

2. Distribution on the Death of Michael R. Hardy

If MICHAEL R. HARDY should die before the complete distribution of his trust share, his trust shall terminate and all of the trust property shall be distributed to such persons, corporations, or other entities, including the beneficiary's own estate, in the manner in which the beneficiary shall elect.

This general power of appointment must be exercised by MICHAEL R. HARDY by either a valid living trust or last will and testament, either of which specifically refers to this power of appointment.

To the extent this general power of appointment is not exercised, my Trustee shall distribute the remaining trust property to MICHAEL R. HARDY's then living descendants, per stirpes.

If MICHAEL R. HARDY has no then living descendants, my Trustee shall distribute the remaining trust property to my then living descendants, per stirpes.

If I have no then living descendants, my Trustee shall distribute the remaining trust property as provided in Item V of this Will.

b. Distribution of Trust Share for Kevin T. Hardy

The trust share for KEVIN T. HARDY shall be held in trust and administered and distributed as follows:

1. Distributions of Net Income and Principal

My Trustee, in its sole and absolute discretion, shall pay to, or apply for the benefit of, KEVIN T. HARDY as much of the net income and principal from his trust share as my Trustee deems advisable for his education, health, maintenance, and support.

When KEVIN T. HARDY reaches the age of 25, or if on the creation of his trust, he has already attained the age of 25, my Trustee shall distribute 1/2 of the trust accumulated net income and principal, as it is then constituted, to KEVIN T. HARDY, free of the trust.

When KEVIN T. HARDY reaches the age of 30, or if on the creation of his trust, he has already attained the age of 30, my Trustee shall distribute the remaining balance of the trust accumulated net income and principal, as it is then constituted, to KEVIN T. HARDY, free of the trust.

2. Distribution on the Death of Kevin T. Hardy

If KEVIN T. HARDY should die before the complete distribution of his trust share, his trust shall terminate and all of the trust property shall be distributed to such persons, corporations, or other entities, including the beneficiary's own estate, in the manner in which the beneficiary shall elect.

This general power of appointment must be exercised by KEVIN T. HARDY by either a valid living trust or last will and testament, either of which specifically refers to this power of appointment.

To the extent this general power of appointment is not

exercised, my Trustee shall distribute the remaining trust property to KEVIN T. HARDY's then living descendants, per stirpes.

If KEVIN T. HARDY has no then living descendants, my Trustee shall distribute the remaining trust property to my then living descendants, per stirpes.

If I have no then living descendants, my Trustee shall distribute the remaining trust property as provided in Item V of this Will.

Section 3.   **Share of a Descendant of a Deceased Child**

Each share set aside for a deceased child who has descendants who survive me shall be distributed or administered as follows:

a   Outright Distribution

The shares set aside for a deceased child who has descendants who survive me shall be distributed to such descendants, per stirpes.

b.   Retention of a Minor's or Disabled Descendant's Portion in Trust

If any portion of a share is distributable under this Section to any descendant of a deceased child who is under 21 years of age, or to any such descendant who is disabled or incapacitated as defined in Item IX of this Will, then my Trustee shall retain that descendant's share in a separate trust until he or she attains 21 years of age, or until his or her legal disability has ceased, as follows:

1. Distributions of Trust Income and Principal

My Trustee shall pay to or apply for the benefit of the beneficiary as much of the net income and principal of the trust as my Trustee, in its sole and absolute discretion, deems necessary or advisable for the beneficiary's education, health, maintenance, and support.

Any net income not distributed to a beneficiary shall be accumulated and added to principal.

2. Termination and Distribution

My Trustee shall distribute the trust property to a beneficiary:

When he or she attains 21 years of age, or

When he or she ceases to be disabled.

3. A Beneficiary's General Power to Appoint Trust Property

If a beneficiary should die before the complete distribution of his or her trust, the trust shall terminate and all of the trust property shall be distributed to such persons, corporations, or other entities, including the beneficiary's own estate, in the manner in which the beneficiary shall elect.

This general power of appointment must be exercised by the beneficiary by either a valid living trust or last will and testament, either of which specifically refers to this power of appointment.

To the extent this general power of appointment is not

exercised, my Trustee shall distribute the remaining trust property to the then living descendants of the beneficiary, per stirpes.

If the beneficiary has no then living descendants, my Trustee shall distribute the remaining trust property to my then living descendants, per stirpes.

If I have no then living descendants, my Trustee shall distribute the remaining trust property as provided in Item V of this Will.

ITEM V

Ultimate Distribution Pattern

If at any time there is no person, corporation, or other entity entitled to receive all or any part of my property (including property from testamentary trusts, lapsed legacies and devises):

One-half of the property shall be distributed to those persons who would be my heirs had I then died intestate owning such property.

The balance of the property shall be distributed to those persons who would be my spouse's heirs had my spouse then died intestate owning such property.

The distribution of property, for purposes of this Item, shall be determined by the laws of descent and distribution for intestate estates in the State of Georgia as such laws are in effect at the time of any distribution under this Item.

ITEM VI

Naming the Executor and Trustee

The provisions for naming the Executor and Executor succession are set forth below:

a. Naming an Individual Executora.

I hereby nominate, constitute, and appoint as Executor of this my Last Will and Testament my spouse, MARY HARDY and direct that she shall serve without bond.

b. Naming Individual Successor Executorb.

If MARY HARDY should fail to qualify as Executor hereunder, or for any reason should cease to act in such capacity, the successor or substitute Executor who shall also serve without bond shall be my sister-in-law, SUZANNE TAYLOR of Atlanta, Georgia.

c. Naming the Trustee

I hereby nominate, constitute, and appoint as Trustee under this my Last Will and Testament my sister-in-law, SUZANNE TAYLOR and direct that she shall serve without bond. If SUZANNE TAYLOR is unable to serve, or cannot continue to serve then a majority of the beneficiaries then eligible to receive mandatory or discretionary distributions of net income under this Will shall forthwith name a Trustee.

If a majority of the beneficiaries then eligible to receive mandatory or discretionary distributions of net income under this Will cannot agree on a Trustee, any beneficiary can petition a court of competent jurisdiction, ex parte, to designate a Trustee.

ITEM VII

Relief From Bonds and Filing Returns

Neither my Executor nor my Trustee shall be required to file any inventory or appraisal or any annual or other returns or reports to any court or to give bond, but shall furnish a statement of receipts and disbursements at least annually to each person then entitled to income from my estate.

ITEM VIII

Powers for Executor and Trustee

By way of illustration and not of limitation and in addition to the powers granted to Executors and Trustees in Official Code of Georgia Annotated Section 53-12-232 as amended to the date of execution of this Will, which powers are incorporated by reference herein, my Executor and my Trustee are specifically authorized and empowered with respect to any property, real or personal, at any time held under any provision of this my Will: to allot, allocate between principal and income, assign, borrow, buy, care for, collect, compromise claims, contract with respect to, continue any business of mine, convey, convert, deal with, dispose of, enter into, exchange, hold, improve, incorporate any business of mine, invest, lease, manage, mortgage, grant and exercise options with respect to, take possession of, pledge, receive, release, repair, sell, sue for, to make distributions or divisions in cash or in kind or partly in each without regard to the income tax basis of such asset, and in general, to exercise all the powers in the management of my Estate or in the management of any trust created by this Will which any individual could exercise in the management of similar property owned in his or her own right, upon such terms and conditions as to my Executor or Trustee may seem best, and to execute and deliver any and all instruments and to do all acts which my Executor or Trustee may deem proper or necessary to carry out the purposes of this my Will, without being limited in any way by the specific grants of power made, and without the necessity of a court order.

ITEM IX

Definitions

For purposes of this Will, the following words and phrases shall be defined as follows:

a. Adopted and Afterborn Persons

For purposes of this Will, adopted persons shall be treated as though they were the natural born children of their adopting parents.

A child in gestation who is later born alive shall be considered a child in being throughout the period of gestation.

b. Descendants

The descendants of a person shall include all of his or her lineal descendants through all generations.

Persons who are legally adopted before age 18 shall be considered natural born children of their adopting parents.

c. Per Stirpes Distributions

Whenever a distribution is to be made to a person's descendants per stirpes, the distributable assets are to be divided into as many shares as there are then living children of such person and deceased children of such person who left then living descendants. Each then living child shall receive one share and the share of each deceased child shall be divided among such child's then living descendants in the same manner.

d. Disability

For purposes of this Will, an individual may be treated as disabled or legally incapacitated if (1) the individual has been declared or adjudicated as such by an appropriate court, or (2) a guardian or conservator has been appointed for the individual by an appropriate court. An individual may also be treated as disabled or legally incapacitated if so certified in writing by at least two medical doctors licensed to practice medicine in the United States.

ITEM X

Simultaneous Death Provision

If any beneficiary and I should die under such circumstances as would make it doubtful whether the beneficiary or I died first, then it shall be conclusively presumed for the purposes of this Will that the beneficiary predeceased me.

ITEM XI

Spendthrift Provision

Except as otherwise provided herein, all payments of principal and income payable, or to become payable, to the beneficiary of any trust created hereunder shall not be subject to anticipation, assignment, pledge, sale or transfer in any manner, nor shall any beneficiary have the power to anticipate or encumber such interest, nor shall such interest, while in the possession of my fiduciary hereunder, be liable for, or subject to, the debts, contracts, obligations, liabilities or torts of any beneficiary.

ITEM XII

Appointment of a Testamentary Guardian

If my spouse shall predecease me, or if my spouse dies after my death without having appointed a testamentary guardian for any minor child or children of ours, then I hereby nominate, constitute, and appoint my sister-in-law, SUZANNE TAYLOR, as testamentary guardian of the person and the property of such minor child or children and to the extent allowed by law direct that such guardian shall serve without bond.

Testimonium Clause

IN WITNESS WHEREOF, I have hereunto set my hand and affixed my seal to this my Last Will and Testament this 15th day of February, 2000.

      s/ John Hardy_____(SEAL)
       JOHN HARDY

Attestation Clause

This Will was, in our presence, signed, sealed, published and declared by JOHN HARDY as and for his Last Will and Testament; and each of us, at his request and in his presence, and in the presence of each other, have hereunto subscribed his or her name as witness the day and year above set out.

s/ _James R. Attorney_____(SEAL)   145 Peachtree Street

Atlanta, GA 30303

s/ _Tina S. Legal Assistant___(SEAL)   145 Peachtree Street

Atlanta, GA 30303

PROOF OF WILL

STATE OF GEORGIA
COUNTY OF FULTON

Before me, the undersigned authority, on this day personally appeared
JOHN HARDY, James R. Attorney and Tina S. Legal Assistant, known
to me to be the testator and the witnesses, respectively, whose names
are subscribed to the annexed or foregoing instrument in their respec-
tive capacities, and, all of said persons being by me duly sworn, JOHN
HARDY, Testator, declared to me and to the said witnesses in my presence that said instrument is his Last Will and Testament and that he
had willingly made and executed it as his free act and deed for the
purposes therein expressed. The witnesses, each on his oath, stated to
me in the presence and hearing of the Testator that the Testator had
declared to them that the instrument is his Last Will and Testament
and that he executed same as much and wanted each of them to sign
the same as witness in the presence of the Testator and at his request;
that he was at that time 18 years of age or older and was of sound
mind; and that each of said witnesses was then at least 18 years of age.

s/ John Hardy
JOHN HARDY, Testator

s/ James R. Attorney
Witness

s/ Tina S. Legal Assistant
Witness

Sworn to and subscribed before me by JOHN HARDY, Testator and
sworn to and subscribed before me by James R. Attorney and Tina S.
Legal Assistant, witnesses, this 15th day of February, 2000.

s/ Susan A. Notary
Notary Public
My Commission Expires: 7-15-03

APPENDIX B

Financial Questionnaires

We have found that the best way to have a productive first meeting is for our new clients to complete and return a questionnaire in advance. Your estate planning attorney needs to know about your family, your assets and what you want to do, before designing your plan.

Approximate amounts are sufficient, and you don't need to spend more than 15 minutes completing the financial questionnaire. Your attorney is particularly looking for assets that are titled in joint tenancy with right of survivorship, because Wills and living trusts have no control over assets titled this way. The information contained on the financial questionnaire also alerts your attorney to estate tax and life insurance problems.

You have permission to copy and enlarge the financial questionnaires.

FINANCIAL QUESTIONNAIRE
For Married Couples

	Address/ Description	How Title Held	Market Value
1. Real Property: a. _____		_____	$_____
b. _____		_____	$_____
c. _____		_____	$_____

2. Promissory Notes: $_____

3. Investments: How is ownership held?
    a. Limited Partnerships   Joint ___ Separate___ $_____
    b. Cash accounts   Joint ___ Separate___ $_____
                               Joint ___ Separate___ $_____
    c. Stocks, bonds   Joint ___ Separate___ $_____

4. Current Value of:
    a. Retirement Plans   Husband $_____
                               Wife $_____
    b. Annuities   Joint __ Separate__ $_____

5. If you own your own business, indicate type, value and owner:
    Sole Proprietor ___   Corporation ___ Other ___ $_____

6. Life Insurance: (Indicate death benefit)
    Company   Owner of Policy   Beneficiary
a._____   _____   _____ $_____
b._____   _____   _____ $_____

7. Please estimate the value of your personal effects $_____
8. Fair market value of other assets $_____
9. Please indicate your total debt (including mortgage) $_____

PLEASE BRING COPIES OF YOUR WILL, TRUST (if you have one) AND DEEDS TO OUR FIRST MEETING.
These will be reviewed during the discussion of your personal situation.

FINANCIAL QUESTIONNAIRE
For Single Persons

	Address/ Description	How Title Held	Market Value
1. Real Property: a.	_____	_____	$_____
b.	_____	_____	$_____
c.	_____	_____	$_____

2. Promissory Notes: $_____

3. Investments: How is ownership held?

   a. Limited Partnerships   Joint ___ Separate___ $_____

   b. Cash accounts   Joint ___ Separate___ $_____

                    Joint ___ Separate___ $_____

   c. Stocks, bonds   Joint ___ Separate___ $_____

4. Current Value of:

   a. Retirement Plans $_____

   b. Annuities $_____

5. If you own your own business, indicate type, value and owner:

   Sole Proprietor ___ Corporation ___ Other ___ $_____

6. Life Insurance: (Indicate death benefit)

   Company   Owner of Policy   Beneficiary

a._____ _____ _____ $_____

b._____ _____ _____ $_____

7. Please estimate the value of your personal effects $_____

8. Fair market value of other assets $_____

9. Please indicate your total debt (including mortgage) $_____

PLEASE BRING COPIES OF YOUR WILL, TRUST (if you have one) AND DEEDS TO OUR FIRST MEETING.

These will be reviewed during the discussion of your personal situation.

APPENDIX C

Instructions for Children*

Section 5. My Philosophy and Guidance for My Children, My Trustees and the Guardian of My Children

MARY and I have spent a great deal of time thinking about what to write in the way of instructions for our children's care and upbringing. These instructions will also apply to any other children MARY and I may have after this document is signed.

After considerable discussion, we realized that although our instructions might be important, they are of little value if the persons carrying them out are not loving and caring. We have put our emphasis on the selection of SUZANNE TAYLOR as guardian and Trustee, because she has values and ideals similar to our own. We believe that SUZANNE will eagerly consult our philosophy in carrying out the administration of the various trusts.

---

* Printed with the permission of Robert A. Goldman, Attorney at Law, 100 Larkspur Landing Circle, Suite 112, Larkspur, CA 94939

To the Guardian of My Children:

In my Will I have designated my sister-in-law SUZANNE TAYLOR, as the guardian of my minor children.

SUZANNE, I picked you as my children's guardian because I know you will love MICHAEL and KEVIN and any other children I may have in the future as though they were your own. The critical issue is love. I know you will impart your wisdom and values to my children and give them every opportunity to grow and develop their potential.

Please give my children the same religious training that you are giving yours. A religious upbringing is important to me and I know that your feeling is the same.

SUZANNE, I know your house is not large enough for my children to have their own rooms. It is important to me that Kevin and Michael each have their own separate room. Therefore I have provided enough funds for you to make an addition to your house or move into a larger house.

A good education is very important to me. I have provided enough funds to pay for tuition for Kevin and Michael to attend private school at least until they reach high school. I want them to be able to devote time to their studies. If they want to work during high school I prefer that they work on the weekends and not on school days. The schools they attend should have the highest academic standards so that they will always be challenged and well prepared for admission to the best colleges.

I want my children to visit their grandparents for a few weeks every summer, preferably at the family farm in Kentucky. Please arrange and pay for their transportation.

Make sure that my children receive their allowance every Saturday. KEVIN and MICHAEL receive the same amount. Be liberal with the amount paid to them for their allowance.

Encourage KEVIN and MICHAEL to play a musical instrument and participate in the school's band or orchestra programs. Pay for private music lessons, if they show a real interest in the lessons and practicing.

I want KEVIN and MICHAEL to play as much baseball (or any other sport they should become interested in) as they want. I believe it is important to develop their bodies and a lifelong commitment to physical exercise. Always encourage them to participate in athletics and display good sportsmanship.

Teach my children about their roots, and gradually give them wings so they will be independent and productive members of the community when they become adults.

To KEVIN and MICHAEL
and Any Other Children I May Have in the Future:

Education is very important to me. I encourage you to seek and obtain advanced degrees. I direct my Trustee and your guardian to offer you every opportunity to pursue higher education whether it be in physics or philosophy, computer science or chemistry, marine biology or medicine. Be it a Ph.D. in history, literature, physics, or mathematics, or an M.D., D.D.S., or J.D., the doctorate is worth obtaining. Strive to obtain it, not from any school, but from a respected institution, preferably one outstanding in your field of endeavor.

A true education will extend beyond formal training. I have tried to instill in you a love of books and a thirst for knowledge.

I do not want you to focus your life on making money. That is not a legitimate purpose in life — to make as much money as you can. Find something you really love to do, and make that your life's work. I ask both of you, and any other children I may have in the future, to be responsible. You must learn to take care of yourself. Take care of your family. Help other people who are less fortunate than you. Make your life's work something positive in the eyes of God.

It is important to work hard, but also, you must spend time with your own children. If you do choose to be successful as an entrepreneur, then by all means, I wish you success, and encourage that, too.

KEVIN and MICHAEL, you know that I love each one of you dearly. To have a happy, fulfilling and satisfying life, a life where you can leave your mark on this world, all you need to do is have compassion, humility, modesty and perform acts of kindness.

To My Trustee:

I have included these thoughts in my trust to inspire my children and offer general guidance to you as their guardian and Trustee. When making distributions to my children, it is my desire that you take these thoughts into consideration and consult my philosophy in carrying out the administration of their trusts.

I want the wishes I have described in this Section carried out until in your sole discretion there is a genuine financial reason as to why my wishes are not reasonable.

APPENDIX D

Professional Estate Planning Organizations

American College of Trust and Estate Counsel
3415 South Sepulveda Blvd.
Suite 330
Los Angeles, CA 90034
Phone (310) 398-1888
Fax (310) 572-7280
www.actec.org

National Academy of Elder Law Attorneys, Inc.
1604 North Country Club Rd.
Tucson, AZ 85116
Phone (520) 881-4005
Fax (520) 325-7925
www.naela.com

National Association of Estate Planners and Councils
270 S. Bryn Mawr Ave.
P.O. Box 46
Bryn Mawr, PA 19010-2196
Phone (610) 526-1389
Fax (610) 526-1310
www.naepc.org

National Network of Estate Planning Attorneys, Inc.
One Valmont Plaza, Fourth Floor
Omaha, NE 68154-5203
Phone (800) 638-8681
Fax (402) 964-3800
www.netplanning.com

GLOSSARY

401(k) account — an employer record maintained for each 401(k) plan participant that keeps the income, gains and losses of each participant separate.

401(k) plan — a type of tax advantaged retirement plan created by an employer to benefit its employees.

activities of daily living — getting out of bed, walking to the bathroom, using the toilet, bathing, eating, and dressing.

adjusted taxable gifts — the sum of each calendar years' taxable gifts.

alternative approach to estate planning — the estate planning method promoted in this book. This method is based on educating the client about all the available goals, and then having the client decide precisely what he wants his estate plan to accomplish.

annual gift tax exclusion — the $11,000 amount (as adjusted for inflation) that you can give annually to an unlimited number of persons without incurring a gift tax.

annuity — a contract between an individual and an insurance company whereby the individual transfers money to the insurance company, and the insurance company promises to pay the money back in installments at some future date, usually at retirement.

applicable credit amount — the amount, formerly called the unified credit, that is subtracted from a taxpayer's gift or estate tax due. In 2003, the applicable credit amount was $345,800.

applicable exclusion amount — the value of assets ($1 million in 2003) that the applicable credit amount ($345,000 in 2003) shelters from the gift tax or estate tax and that can be passed on gift tax free or estate tax free. For the estate tax, the applicable exclusion amount is $1 million in 2003 and gradually increases to $3.5 million by 2009. For the gift tax, the applicable exclusion amount remains fixed at $1 million, and will be indexed for inflation beginning in 2010.

articles of organization — the document filed with a state agency, usually the Secretary of State, to form a limited liability company.

asset protection planning — legally organizing assets in advance to safeguard them against claims of future creditors.

assignment agreement — a short document that is used to transfer personal and household effects (e.g., jewelry, clothes, and furniture) to a revocable living trust.

beneficiary — the person for whose benefit a trust is created.

bypass trust — same as Family Trust.

capital asset — property such as securities, coin collections, etc., that you own for investment or personal purposes.

capital gains rate — the federal income tax rate that applies to gains from the sale of a capital asset. Generally, the maximum capital gains rate for individuals is 15% for assets held more than one year. Corporations do not receive special tax rates for capital gains

cash value life insurance — life insurance that is intended to last for your lifetime.

charitable lead trust — an irrevocable trust whose income is paid to charities for a term of years. At the expiration of the term, the remaining trust assets are paid to non-charitable beneficiaries, usually children or grandchildren. Its purpose is to eliminate estate tax on property in the trust upon the death of the trust maker, and eventually pass the original trust assets to children and grandchildren.

charitable remainder trust — an irrevocable trust that is used to avoid the capital gains tax on the sale of highly appreciated assets. Typically, the trust's assets are paid to the trust maker and his spouse for life, and upon the surviving spouse's death, the remaining trust property is paid to a charitable beneficiary.

charitable split dollar life insurance program — an income and estate tax avoidance strategy, popular in the 1990's, that was outlawed by Congress in 1999.

children's trust — an irrevocable trust created for a minor or adult child. It can be a separate document that comes into existence while the trust maker is living, or it can be a part of a Will or revocable living trust that comes into existence after the testator's or trust maker's death.

civil law — the legal system handed down from the Romans that is based on written legal codes. Louisiana, Quebec, most of continental Europe and Latin America have civil law systems with modern legal codes. In the U.S., civil law also refers to the laws that govern our dealings with each other such as family law and contract law, but does not include criminal law.

common law — the great body of English law too massive to be written down in one place that was slowly developed by judges over several centuries. Though legislation has modified some parts and made other parts obsolete, common law (as modified by legislation) is still followed in the world's English speaking countries.

Common Trust — a trust for minor children that comes into existence upon the death of the surviving spouse. Typically when the youngest child completes college, the remaining assets of the Common Trust are transferred in equal shares to a separate trust for each child.

community property states — Louisiana, Texas, Arizona, New Mexico, Nevada, California, Idaho, Washington and Wisconsin. In these states, assets acquired during a marriage (other than gifts and inheritances) are presumed to be owned half by the husband and half by the wife. You cannot sell your half of the community property or give it away, but upon your death you can leave it to anyone you choose under the terms of your Will or revocable living trust.

corporation — historically, the most common entity formed under state law to conduct business. A corporation's shareholders (i.e., owners) are not personally liable for the corporation's debts.

co-trustee — a person (individual or institution) who shares fiduciary powers with another trustee.

coupon amount — the term used in this book as a synonym (a word having a similar meaning as another word) for the applicable exclusion amount.

custodial care — the type of assistance required by a person who needs help bathing, eating, dressing, etc. Don't confuse with skilled nursing care where assistance is provided to people with much heavier care needs.

decedent — a person who died.

disclaimer — a legal means that allows an heir to refuse to accept an inheritance; it is often used in estate tax planning to allow the surviving spouse to direct assets to the first spouse to die's Family Trust and to exclude those assets from the estate tax.

donee — the person who receives a gift.

donor — the person who makes a gift.

durable power of attorney — a document where one person (the principal) appoints another person (the agent) to act on his behalf and manage his affairs. The agent's authority continues even though the principal becomes mentally incapacitated. The agent's authority terminates upon the principal's death.

dynasty trust — an irrevocable trust that allows assets to pass from one generation to the next without incurring an estate tax or a generation-skipping tax.

estate — all the assets an individual owns or controls while living or at death. Also means an individual's probate estate.

estate planning — a plan to protect yourself, your family, and your assets while you are alive and after your death. More specifically, the field that solves the issues listed on pages 50 and 51 of this book.

estate tax — a tax that is imposed on a decedent's taxable estate. The Internal Revenue Code states that the federal estate tax "is imposed on the transfer of the taxable estate of every decedent who is either a U.S. citizen or a resident." The word "transfer" has little significance since it is presumed that a decedent's taxable estate will be transferred.

exclusion amount — same as applicable exclusion amount.

executor — the individual or institution named in a Will or named by a probate court to carry out the terms of a Will and to settle the decedent's estate. In some states the executor is called the personal representative.

family foundation — an advanced tax savings strategy whereby assets are transferred during life or at death to a charitable or educational organization, usually controlled by one donor or one family; also known as a private foundation.

family limited partnership — an advanced estate tax savings strategy that uses a limited partnership to transfer assets to younger family members.

Family Trust — a trust created by a married person for the purpose of excluding assets from the federal estate tax. The Family Trust that comes into existence is the one written into the Will or revocable living trust of the first spouse to die. It provides income and discretionary distributions of principal for the surviving spouse, but no estate tax is imposed on the Family Trust's assets when the surviving spouse dies. It is also called the unified credit trust, bypass trust or Trust B.

fee simple — a type of property ownership that means you own the entire asset all by yourself. You can sell the asset, give it away, or upon your death you can leave it under the terms of your Will or revocable living trust.

fiduciary — a trustee, executor or guardian.

fiduciary powers — the authority granted to a fiduciary under state law or under a Will or trust.

Form 706 — the United States Estate (and Generation-Skipping Transfer) Tax Return. The return must be filed for every U.S. citizen or resident decedent whose gross estate on the date of death exceeds the applicable exclusion amount.

fraudulent conveyance — a transfer of assets made with the intent to hinder, delay or defraud current creditors.

fully funded living trust — a revocable living trust that contains all the trust maker's assets other than his retirement plan assets.

funding — the process of transferring assets to a revocable living trust. Technically the assets are titled in the name of the Trustee(s) for the benefit of the trust beneficiary.

general partnership — a business carried on by two or more persons, as co-owners, for profit. Each partner is personally liable for all claims against the partnership.

general power of appointment — a common provision found in many trusts that gives a trust beneficiary upon his death, the right to redirect trusts assets to anyone he chooses, including his own creditors. For estate tax purposes the value of the property subject to a general power of appointment is included in the trust beneficiary's gross estate.

generation-skipping tax — a federal tax on transfers to grandchildren or anyone (other than a spouse) 37 ½ years younger than the donor. The intent of the tax is to force individuals to pass assets to their children, rather than their grandchildren, so that the estate tax can be applied to each generation. The tax does not affect most people because every donor has a $1 million (as adjusted for inflation) lifetime generation-skipping tax exemption.

gift tax — the federal tax that is imposed on gifts made during your lifetime.

gross estate — the value of all assets of a decedent subject to the federal estate tax.

guardian — the person appointed by a local probate court to be in charge of a minor (a person under the age of 18) or a mentally disabled adult.

guardian of the property — the person appointed by a local probate court to be in charge of the assets of a minor (a person under the age of 18) or a mentally disabled adult. In some states a guardian of the property is called a conservator.

inside creditors — creditors of your business.

Internal Revenue Code — the text of the United States tax laws that deals with income, estate, gift, employment and excise taxes, along with the procedural and administrative provisions.

inventory — a list of all the decedent's assets that the executor may be required to file with the probate court within four to six month's after the decedent's death.

IRA — a tax advantaged retirement account that can be created by salary or wage earners; also called an individual retirement account.

irrevocable life insurance trust — an estate tax savings strategy that uses an irrevocable trust to keep life insurance proceeds from being subject to the federal estate tax.

irrevocable trust — a trust that cannot be changed by the trust maker. It is treated as a separate entity for tax purposes.

joint revocable living trust — a single revocable living trust created by a married couple to benefit both spouses. Joint living trusts are commonly used in community property states (other than Louisiana), but may also be used in all the other states.

joint tenancy — same as joint tenancy with right of survivorship.

joint tenancy with right of survivorship — a type of property ownership often used by spouses and family members. The unusual feature is that when one joint owner dies his share automatically passes to the surviving owner(s). The real owner is the last one living. You can sell your interest in the asset or give it away, but upon your death you cannot leave it to anyone under the terms of your Will or revocable living trust.

This form of ownership produces odd results. Let's assume there are three owners whose property is titled in joint tenancy with right of survivorship. For purposes of a creditor's claim, each owner owns 100% of the property, and a creditor can take the entire property to satisfy a debt of one of the joint owners. However, if one of the three joint owners wants to make a gift of his interest to anyone he chooses, he can give away only one-third of the property. The donee (the person who receives a gift) of the one-third interest becomes a tenant in common. And the other two owners own two-thirds of the property with each other as joint tenants with right of survivorship.

JTWROS — a shorthand way that financial institutions use to indicate joint tenancy with right of survivorship.

LLC — the shorthand name for a limited liability company.

limited liability company (LLC) — a relatively new type of business entity created under state law that possesses features of both corporations and partnerships.

limited partnership — a partnership created under state law that has both general and limited partners. The general partners control the day-to-day operations of the partnership and are personally liable for all partnership debts. The limited partners do not control the business operations and are liable for partnership debts only to the extent of their investment in the partnership.

living trust — a trust that comes into existence while you are living. In this book living trust is used as the shortened name for revocable living trust.

long-term care insurance — insurance to pay the costs of care when you are cognitively (mentally) impaired or can no longer perform the everyday living skills people ordinarily perform without help (such as bathing, dressing and eating).

marital deduction — a gift tax deduction or an estate tax deduction that is given to an individual who transfers assets to his spouse.

Marital Trust — a trust created by a married person for two purposes: (1) to guarantee that upon the surviving spouse's death the trust assets will pass to the children, and (2) to delay the imposition of the estate tax until the surviving spouse's death. The Marital Trust that comes into existence is the one written into the Will or revocable living trust of the first spouse to die. It provides income and principal for the surviving spouse, and the Marital Trust's assets are subject to the federal estate tax upon the surviving spouse's death.

Medicaid — the jointly funded Federal and state medical assistance program for the financially needy.

Medicare — the Federal government health insurance program for persons 65 years and older, and for some others who are disabled.

membership interest certificates — the name for a limited liability company's stock certificates.

operating agreement — the written agreement between a limited liability company's "president", called the manager, and the "owners", called the members, that defines which of these two groups controls the operations of the company. An operating agreement can be written to provide asset protection and estate tax savings for the limited liability company's members.

outside creditors — your non-business, personal creditors.

person — an individual, estate, trust or corporation.

pour-over Will — the Will prepared as a companion to a revocable living trust. The main purpose of this Will, other than naming a guardian for minor children, is to distribute the decedent's assets to his living trust.

power of attorney — a document where one person (the principal) appoints another person (the agent) to act on his behalf and manage his affairs. The agent's authority terminates when the principal becomes mentally incapacitated or dies.

power of appointment — a trust provision that allows a spouse or child to decide where trust assets go long after the trust maker dies.

probate — the legal process of proving the validity of a Will; the executor's job is to pay a decedent's probate estate to the decedent's creditors and Will beneficiaries.

probate estate — all the assets an individual owns at the time of his death whose disposition is controlled by his Will. It does not include assets owned by a revocable living trust; assets titled in joint tenancy with right of survivorship; and assets such as life insurance and 401(k) accounts whose beneficiary is a person other than an estate.

qualified personal residence trust — A special type of irrevocable trust used in saving estate taxes. You make a gift of your residence or vacation home to the trust, and you continue to live in your home for the number of years (the "term") you choose. Afterward, your home belongs to the trust beneficiaries, usually your children. The gift of your home to the trust is ignored, and your home is included in your taxable estate if you die before the term is over.

revocable living trust — a trust that can be changed by the trust maker up until his death. In this book revocable living trust and living trust are used interchangeably.

separate property — in community property states, assets a spouse owns before the marriage and inheritances, gifts, and personal injury recoveries a spouse receives during the marriage.

simple trust — an irrevocable trust that requires all of its income to be distributed annually, has no charitable beneficiaries, and does not make a distribution of principal during the year. Whether a trust is a simple trust is determined on a yearly basis.

simple Will — a Will that says, "I leave everything to my spouse if she survives me, and if she does not survive me, then to my children."

skilled nursing care — assistance provided or supervised by a registered nurse or physician, such as administering oxygen, giving intravenous injections, treating wounds, and using a feeding tube.

sole proprietor — the individual who owns the assets of a business in his own name.

sole proprietorship — a business in which an individual owns all the business assets in his own name.

step-up in basis — The Internal Revenue Code contains specific rules on how to compute gain on the sale of an asset. Generally gain is determined by subtracting the cost of an asset from its selling price. Under the step-up in basis tax provision, the "cost" (sometimes called the basis) of an asset you inherit is its fair market value on the date of the decedent's death. The result is that an asset sold soon after you inherit it will have little or no gain.

taxable estate — a decedent's gross estate for federal estate tax purposes less the allowable deductions, which mainly include mortgages, other debts, funeral expenses, attorney's fees, executor's fees, charitable bequests, and bequests to a spouse.

taxable gifts — the total amount of gifts made during the calendar year less any annual gift tax exclusions, and deductions for marital gifts and charitable gifts.

tenants in common — a common way to own an asset with one or more other people. Each owner owns a fractional interest in the asset, which is called an undivided interest. You can sell your interest in the asset, give it away, or upon your death you can leave it to anyone you choose under the terms of your Will or revocable living trust.

term life insurance — life insurance that lasts for a certain term or time period.

testamentary trust — an irrevocable trust created in a Will by a testator. A testamentary trust does not come into existence until the testator dies and his Will has been probated.

testator — an individual who makes a Will before he dies. Traditionally, testator refers to a male and testatrix refers to a female.

traditional approach to estate planning — the attorney decides what the client needs without discussing the client's goals.

trust — a written contract between the trust maker and the trustee to hold and manage assets for the benefit of others (one or more beneficiaries).

Trust A — another name for the Marital Trust.

Trust B — another name for the Family Trust.

trust income — The exact definition is determined from reading the trust agreement. Interest income and dividends are the most common types of trust income. A portion of the ordinary income of a limited liability company (LLC) or partnership can also be trust income if the trust owns a part of the LLC or partnership. Trust income does not include capital gains unless the trust specifically requires this. For trust accounting purposes capital gains are usually added to trust principal, rather than to trust income.

trust maker — the person (more commonly called the grantor or settlor) who creates a trust to hold and manage all or a portion of his assets. As a point of semantics, a trust maker does not create a testamentary trust. A testamentary trust is created in a Will by a testator.

trustee — the individual or institution that holds trust property for the benefit of the trust's beneficiaries.

unified credit — another name for the applicable credit amount.

unified credit trust — another name for the Family Trust or Trust B.

Will — a legal document that disposes of the assets you own at your death.

SUGGESTED READING

Beyond Death & Taxes, A Guide to Total Wealth Control, Essential Edition by Gregory J. Englund. Boston: Estate Planning Press, 2002 Revision. (This short guide explains advanced estate tax planning strategies in terms that are easy to understand. It can be ordered directly from the publisher 1-617-439-5266.)

Beyond the Grave: The Right and Wrong Way of Leaving Money to your Children by Gerald Condon and Jeffrey Condon. Toronto: HarperBusiness, 1996. (This book provides a detailed look at strategies (and their consequences) for passing on wealth to your loved ones and charities.)

Gifting to People You Love by Adriane G. Berg. New York: New Market Press, 1996. (The section on planning for college offers useful information for parents planning for their children's or grandchildren's education.)

The Inheritor's Handbook: A Definitive Guide for Beneficiaries by Dan Rottenberg. Princeton: Bloomberg Press, 1999. (This book gives children practical advice for encouraging their parents to do estate planning. It lists step-by-step instructions on what to do following the death of a parent or spouse. The book also contains helpful advice about managing wealth and choosing banks or other financial institutions as a trustee.)

J.K. Lasser's Choosing the Right Long-Term Care Insurance by Benjamin Lipson.New York: John Wiley & Sons, Inc., 2002.

INDEX

ABOUT THE AUTHORS

Robert Dunn is an attorney whose law practice is devoted to preparing Wills and Trusts, and designing and implementing detailed estate plans. He graduated from the University of Virginia with a B.S. in accounting; earned a law degree from Cumberland School of Law, Samford University; and a Master of Laws in taxation from New York University Graduate School of Law. Robert worked for major accounting firms in New York City until he started his law practice in 1982, in the metropolitan Atlanta area.

Robert has given estate planning seminars to insurance professionals, CPAs and the general public. He is a member of the Atlanta Estate Planning Council, Georgia and Florida Bar Associations and the New York State Society of CPAs.

Robert's philosophy about estate planning evolved through years of attending professional seminars, self-education and working with clients to design and execute their estate plans. He came to realize that many well intentioned but misinformed parents were protecting their families with Wills that were either worthless pieces of paper or that would accomplish considerably less than they expected. Although there were numerous estate planning books, the word was not getting out. His desire to fill this void provided the impetus for this book.

Joan Dorfman works with Robert as his legal assistant. She earned her undergraduate degree from Cornell University, and Masters degrees from the University of Arizona and Georgia State University.

Robert and Joan are married, and live in Alpharetta, Georgia with their three children.